What Readers Are Saying About

Prayers for the Mother of the Bride

"Traci Matt writes like a friend dedicated to helping you make the most of your daughter's wedding. As you draw near to God with these beautifully written prayers, you will find yourself strengthened by the truth and relieved by His abundant grace. Within each chapter, you will discover new ways to communicate with God which will enhance not only the upcoming wedding, but also the rest of your life."

> - Jennifer O. White, author of *Prayers for New Brides* and *Hope for Your Marriage*

"During a blessed yet painful life transition, Traci Matt gives words for the unutterable groans of a mother's heart. With compassion, care, and optimism, Traci walks us from motherhood to Mother of the Bride to Jesus' feet. This book is a treasured devotional for this tender time."

> - Lea Ann Garfias, mother and author of *Rocking Ordinary* and *Homeschool Made Easy*

"Traci has a beautiful way of helping mothers prepare for the marriage of their daughters. The beautiful truths from the Word of God have been woven into each devotion with love and care. I know this will be a treasured resource that can be passed down to generations to come."

> - Kimberly Dewberry, blogger at "Transforming Normal"

"Reading through *Prayers for the Mother of the Bride* turns wedding planning jitters into an oasis of calm. Traci models wisdom and grace through her writing. My bride-to-be who lives in a different city loves getting my texts about what was prayed for that day. I'm looking forward to greeting the big day with a smile on my face and joy and serenity in my heart.

- Beverly K.

"The beautiful prayers of comfort, wisdom, and encouragement are orchestrated by God. I praise him for that! It is not only a how-to-do-a-wedding book, but more importantly, a comfort in so many ways. It draws me back to what's really happening—the joining of two precious people standing and committing before God. In addition to being spiritually uplifting to me at this crazy time, it's also an organized reminder of things to think about and complete. As I read, I'm reminded of Isaiah 50:4 and it definitely applies to these devotionals: 'The Sovereign Lord has given me a well-instructed tongue, to know the word that sustains the weary. He wakens me morning by morning, wakens my ear to listen like one being instructed.' I will be reading this every day!"

- Gina J.

"This book pointed to Christ and His strength and control over every situation as my daughter and I worked through the challenges of planning a long-distance wedding. Each day's reading encouraged me to keep my focus on Him and to keep the details covered in prayer. Any mother planning a wedding will be tremendously blessed by this book!"

- Bridget B.

Prayers for the Mother of the Bride

Traci Matt

For my beautiful Miss E.

Just the thought of you makes my heart sing.

Table of Contents

Who can describe the transports of a heart truly parental on beholding a daughter shoot up like some fair and modest flower, and acquire, day after day, fresh beauty and growing sweetness, so as to fill every eye with pleasure and every heart with admiration?

James Fordyce

Introduction

Congratulations, Mama—your baby girl is getting married. It may be hard to believe that spunky, inquisitive, beautiful little daughter has already grown into a lovely young woman. She is making plans and dreaming dreams and plotting a future with her man. Your life is about to become a blur of to-do lists, calendar negotiations, fancy meals, and dressing rooms.

You likely envisioned these days of ribbons and lace, laughter and love, even before your daughter did. You remember the times she played "wedding" with dress-up clothes and stuffed animals, while promising to live with you and her daddy forever. You have given advice, dried tears, and shared visions of castles in the air as she entered young adulthood. In recent days, you may be fighting the urge to cry when considering how the words "Who gives this woman?" will become a marker which transforms your family in an instant.

You may be hoping for blissful bonding times with your future son-in-law, bestowing formal blessings on your daughter as she prepares to become a wife, and a little pampering for yourself as the day approaches. The reality may be far from that vision as you attempt to weave those ideals into your already hectic schedule and deal with those who make it hectic. Whether you played a hands-on role in the courtship and engagement, or your mothering has become a long-distance affair, the heavy responsibility and privilege to cover the couple with prayer should now be a key element of your daily life.

Perhaps you are having a hard time celebrating the engagement with your whole heart. Maybe your daughter's choice of spouse or timing is not what you would consider ideal. Your own financial situation or emotional health may not be what you had hoped for at this point in your life. You may even see your daughter making unhealthy decisions with clear ties to mistakes of your own. Regardless of the circumstances, your job is to pray over and support the couple as they begin the beautiful and mysterious task of becoming one.

Similar to the companion volume *Prayers for the Mother of the Groom*, this guide is a two-month countdown to the wedding day. You may begin using it at any point in the planning process, perhaps cycling through it multiple times, depending on the length of the engagement. If you like to journal while praying, feel free to write in the margins or use a notebook to record your specific requests.

If for some reason your family structure does not fit into a traditional picture frame, never fear. Simply follow the Holy Spirit's leading as you consider each day's prayers, adapting them to fit your unique situation. But by all means keep going before God, for no prayer is more heartfelt than that of a mother.

Then as you stand and turn, heart pounding, to watch your precious child begin her bridal march, you can rest in the knowledge that every aspect of her celebration and life to come has been covered in prayer. May God bless you as you begin this odyssey of joyful transformation with your darling daughter.

Something Borrowed

"Shew me thy ways, O Lord; teach me thy paths. Lead me in thy truth, and teach me: for thou art the God of my salvation; on thee do I wait all the day."

Psalm 25: 4-5 (KJV)

Day 60 – Be Still

Believe it or not, stillness will probably need to be scheduled into your life over the coming months. Even if your daughter is an organized and efficient event planner, there will be choice after choice, party after party, and emotion after emotion for you to deal with as these days unfold. Begin now to practice quiet meditation before the Lord by simply coming to him, no list or agenda in hand.

If your burgeoning calendar begins to drain you of energy and joy, turn back to this page and remind yourself where your strength begins: "Be still, and know that I am God: I will be exalted among the heathen, I will be exalted in the earth" Psalm 46:10 (KJV).

Father, help me to heed the instruction the Israelites were quick to dismiss in Isaiah 30:15: "For thus the Lord God, the Holy One of Israel, has said, 'In repentance and rest you will be saved, In quietness and trust is your strength...'" Make me eager to seek your face and hear your voice as I meditate on your word and bask in your tender thoughts toward me and my family. Empower me for the tasks ahead as I honor you with my time.

All-wise God, you know every one of the thoughts which are swirling around in my mind, distracting and sometimes even threatening to suffocate me. Help me to deal with them now, even if I need to write them down and put them aside. (Pause and lay aside your most distracting concerns, either literally or figuratively, before continuing.)

Forgive me for the prideful attitude which drives me to do "just one more thing" before coming to you, as if my efforts will be the key to any success. I confess that you are the key to success and the giver of all good things (James 1:17). Help quiet my mind and heart so I may be able to recognize and thank you for the good you are pouring into my life and that of my family members during these coming weeks. Speak to me now as I rest and focus on you. (Pause here.)

Thank you for the Holy Spirit which dwells in me, communicating clearly the comfort and wisdom you so graciously and lovingly wish me to experience. I pray that any interference from the enemy intended to stir up and distract me from your presence would be stopped. I beg for clear thinking. Thank you for the messages I will hear only by ceasing my activity and listening for you. (Pause one last time.)

I pray for opportunities to encourage my daughter and other family members to plan moments of quiet rest before you. Open my eyes to any chance I have to lighten their loads and give them times to retreat in stillness. Continue to draw us to you as we dash toward the momentous day and the new branch of our family begins to grow. In Christ's name and for his glory, amen.

Something Borrowed

In the silence of the heart God speaks. If you face God
in prayer and silence,

God will speak to you. Then you will know that you
are nothing.

It is only when you realize your nothingness, your
emptiness,

that God can fill you with Himself.

Souls of prayer are souls of great silence.

Mother Teresa

Day 59 – Let Praises Ring

No matter what circumstances you face as you begin planning for this life-changing occasion, your heart's desire is to be rooted and grounded in the love of Christ. What better way to stand firm as you look to these busy days ahead than by praising God for who he is and acknowledging his great loving-kindness. Why not spend the first couple times in pre-wedding prayer on your knees (or in your favorite prayer-posture) in adoration and thanksgiving. You may even want to turn back to this section each day as you intercede for your daughter's wedding, meditating on and loving God just because of who he is. Before you bring one petition to his throne, let heaven ring with praises from your heart.

Almighty God, we praise you for the mystery of who you are. We praise your holy name, and hold it in highest esteem above all other names. Praise you for being all-knowing, all-seeing, and all-powerful, both on earth and in the heavens. Creator God, we praise you for the endless ingenuity and might you displayed when speaking our world into existence; and praise your name as your patient compassion continues to hold it together in perfect balance.

Lord Jesus, we praise you for your strength of obedience in living a grace-defining, sinless life. We praise you for your deep-reaching love which crossed the lines of race, class, and religion during your time on earth, and continues to do so in ways we cannot fathom. Let us rejoice with the angels, Lamb of God, as your atoning work reconciles souls (Luke 15:10). Praise you for being the way, the truth, and the life, and the only path to our heavenly Father (John 14:6).

Holy Spirit, we praise you for your incomparable wisdom and knowledge. Praise you for being the spirit of truth who abides with us, and will be with us (John 14:17). For the patience you lavish on us when we grieve your heart, we praise you. For the tenderness that cares enough to intercede for us before God the father (Romans 8:26), we praise you. For the powerful witness you use to confirm to us that we are children of God (Romans 8:16), we praise you.

Let our hearts join with the psalmist (Psalm 150):

Praise the Lord!

Praise God in His sanctuary;

Praise Him in His mighty expanse.

Praise Him for His mighty deeds;

Praise Him according to His excellent greatness.

Praise Him with trumpet sound;

Praise Him with harp and lyre.

Praise Him with timbrel and dancing;

Praise Him with stringed instruments and pipe.

Praise Him with loud cymbals;

Praise Him with resounding cymbals.

Let everything that has breath praise the Lord.

Praise the Lord!

Amen.

Something Borrowed

Praise consists in the love of God, in wonder at the goodness of God, in recognition of the gifts of God, in seeing God in all things He gives us, ay, and even in the things that He refuses to us; so as to see our whole life in the light of God; and seeing this, to bless Him, adore Him, and glorify Him.

Henry Edward Manning

Day 58 – It's a New Day

What a joy to add another red-letter day to your family's calendar! The question is, which day will they pick? With only 365 calendar squares to choose from, how hard can it be? In addition to clearing their own schedules, the bride and groom must consult with a long list of family and friends, churches and reception halls, as well as special vendors they wish to hire, such as photographers or florists. Then there's the weather, previously scheduled family events, and the important task of choosing the perfect length for their engagement. The flowchart can get pretty complicated! Let's pray they choose wisely.

Father, how can something that sounds so simple have the potential to be so difficult? This will be the first of thousands of decisions my daughter and her future husband will make together over their lifetimes. What an important process it will be. Have mercy on them and on me as I take my place in the scheme of things to come.

First of all, please give the couple unity as they discuss the length of the engagement, and help them choose what is right for them, even if others disagree (even me). Give them clear thinking as they consider the coming months and choose which day they should get married. Help them to be considerate of each other's work or school schedules, as well as those of family and friends.

Bring to mind any potential problems with holidays or other special events already on the calendar. Reveal anything which might be a conflict in our family or the community where the wedding will take place. Give them a realistic picture of potential weather hazards. Allow them creativity to choose a day which is unique to them for some reason. Free up the calendars of those special people they wish to have participate in the ceremony. Open up doors for the perfect venues and vendors to be available. Create the ideal window of time for them to celebrate their honeymoon.

I pray they would remember to consult each of their loved ones, friends, and others they wish to involve in the festivities. May there be no hurt feelings if someone who desires to be at the ceremony has an irresolvable schedule conflict. In Jesus' name, may no bitterness be allowed to grow at any time in this situation, but rather, may strong avenues of grace and honest communication be built.

Once the date is chosen, may there be no unforeseen conflicts which create aggravation or extra expense. If the calendar must be adjusted for some reason, help that process go smoothly. In the end, give the bride and groom grace and courage to choose what works best for them and those they love, to your glory. Amen.

Something Borrowed

To every thing there is a season, and a time to every purpose under the heaven.

Ecclesiastes 3:1 (KJV)

Day 57 – A Firm Foundation

Although all eyes will be on your daughter as she walks down the aisle, many will be watching you throughout the coming weeks. How will you handle it if the seamstress hems your dress too short? Or your daughter announces a post-wedding move across the country? Or the venue suddenly declares bankruptcy the week before the wedding? How can you possibly deal gracefully with any unexpected hiccups when you are facing such an emotionally-charged life change? Stressors—large and small—may threaten your mood and peace of mind, but they don't have to control you. Scripture tells us in 1 Corinthians 2:16 that believers "have the mind of Christ." Claim that mind of peace and clarity today and each day, and your perspective will stay healthy no matter the circumstances.

Begin now to focus on a passage or memorize a key verse or two which provide peace in the turmoil. Ask close friends and family to pray for you in very specific ways. Make it your desire to be different in the face of stress, and perhaps even cause people to ask what makes you different. Then be prepared to offer a reason for the hope that is in you (1 Peter 3:15).

Lord, thank you for being my peace. Thank you for the solid assurance that you are love, and your perfect love casts out any fear I may experience as this wedding process continues to unfold (1 John 4:18). As this anxiety may appear in many forms – fear of losing control, fear of losing my daughter, fear of unforeseen expenses, fear of unpleasant family interactions – help me to quickly recognize and cast it out in your name.

I ask for mercy as I endeavor to keep your word and your spirit foremost in my mind at all times. Give me the desire and opportunity to stay grounded in prayer and the reading of Scripture. Provide prayer partners who can lift me up before your throne, and help me to be honest with them about my needs.

As I keep your strong word before me throughout the day, give me clarity to memorize your directives and put them into action. Keep my mind lucid and focused on you even, and particularly, when a situation arises which threatens to make me react in an ungodly fashion. Help me to hear myself as I speak to others and to keep an honest account of times I need to apologize. I may be "only human" but I do not want to use that excuse for overreacting when others are watching my attitudes and behavior as a Christian woman. My desire is to behave in all circumstances as your child.

Please keep me from being self-absorbed. Turn my focus outward to my daughter, husband, and other family members who are also experiencing the ground shifting under their feet during this time of transition. Please provide emotional stability so I might not be a burden when they may be looking to me for strength and comfort.

Protect my mind and heart as I endeavor to please you. In your mighty name, amen.

Something Borrowed

How firm a foundation, ye saints of the Lord,

Is laid for your faith in His excellent Word!

What more can He say than to you He hath said,

You, who unto Jesus for refuge have fled?

How Firm a Foundation, Keene/Kirkham/Keith

Day 56 – The Venue Menu

Has your daughter dreamed of a wedding at your home church, an urban warehouse, or beachside boardwalk ever since she was old enough to walk? Now the addition of another person, and a whole new family, may be complicating those childhood visions. Will the couple choose a spot in the same city as their parents? Do they dream of an exotic destination wedding? Perhaps they want to have a small ceremony and celebrate at a later date with a reception for friends and extended family. The possibilities are endless and have the potential to cause myriad conflicts and hurt feelings. Pray that the bride and groom can find a perfect combination of honoring their families and fulfilling their own dreams for their wedding day.

Lord, first of all I ask that my daughter and future son-in-law would be in complete agreement over where the wedding will take place. If there are special desires one of them has about their wedding day, give them honest communication, but don't let them hold on to childish expectations at the expense of others.

Open up the calendar for any church or venue in which they wish to celebrate. Create a realistic view of what they can afford, and provide reasonably priced options. Help them not to be rushed into any decisions before they are ready, and give them wisdom before they sign contracts or put down deposits. May there be no unforeseen legal entanglements. Provide godly, honest, conscientious people for them to deal with as they make location commitments.

If they happen to choose an outdoor venue, provide a sheltered spot as a Plan B for weather issues, but I beg you to provide lovely weather over our heads that day. If they choose a non-traditional venue, please allow ease of parking and access, especially for any elderly or disabled guests. Provide a safe environment at all times. Provide adequate venue support staff who will operate with loving patience and do nothing but add to our joy that day.

Lord, please go before any disagreements over religious sites, clergy, or service choices. Make this event a time of great spiritual unity and not disunity, regardless of preferences of friends and family. If there are spiritual gaps to be spanned, lavish us with increased understanding and love. May any who would cause dissention in the name of religion excuse themselves from the celebration. May all feel welcome in the location where the wedding takes place. May the love of Christ be my focus regardless where we meet.

Give me the good sense to keep venue opinions to myself unless asked to communicate them. Give me a can-do, flexible attitude even if a choice is made that does not seem best. Give me the strength to act as a positive influence in the marriage starting even at this early stage. Help me to always remember that this is their decision, not mine, and any discomfort or expense will be worth it to see my daughter's face as she first lays eyes on her groom that day. Amen.

Something Borrowed

Take time to deliberate;

but when the time for action arrives,

stop thinking and go in.

Andrew Jackson

Day 55 – It's a Shame

This world is no stranger to shame and its effects. Eve first felt it between her teeth with the fateful bite of forbidden fruit. Since that moment, shame has been a formidable barrier to God's presence. If your daughter carries guilt about poor choices such as sexual missteps, harsh words, broken relationships, or any sort of real or imagined impropriety, the enemy will use that as a way to cloud her thoughts as she plans and enters into marriage. Pray today that no schemes of the forces of darkness would deceive her regarding the fact she is loved and forgiven by the One who gave himself for her. Pray that the Lord's presence would be welcome and delighted in during the weeks to come, and especially as she makes those sacred vows before him.

Heavenly Father, your word tells us clearly that you are a generous forgiver:

"For You, Lord, are good, and ready to forgive, And abundant in lovingkindness to all who call upon You." Psalm 86:5

"Of Him (Jesus Christ) all the prophets bear witness that through His name everyone who believes in Him receives forgiveness of sins." Acts 10:43

"Therefore there is now no condemnation for those who are in Christ Jesus." Romans 8:1

I claim this forgiveness for my family and for myself before we even begin to tackle the plans and decisions in the weeks to come. We desperately need your presence and the peace, wisdom, and joy found there. Saturate our hearts and minds with the assurance of your grace and love. Arrest any attempt of the enemy to keep these days from being the best they can be.

I acknowledge where I have failed as a mother to this young woman; I confess my shortcomings and ask for forgiveness. In your tender mercies, cover my mistakes as only you can. Give me strength to resist ruminating on any shame for those sins covered by the blood of the Lamb.

If my daughter is struggling with any foothold of shame, or even an inkling of false guilt, expose it to the light of your cleansing forgiveness. Keep lies far from her mind. If she needs to sort through any of her past mistakes or sins, provide kind friends and wise counselors to guide her. Likewise I pray for the groom. May he not carry any guilt into the marriage that would provide a rift between their spirits.

As my daughter stands before you to become one with her beloved, may no shame encroach upon her thoughts. Assure her she is clean and new in your eyes. Give her the ability to revel in the moment she becomes a bride. May your overwhelming love be the primary thought in her mind.

May we live like the heavenly royalty we are as children of the Most High God: "For you have not received a spirit of slavery leading to fear again, but you have received a spirit of adoption as sons by which we cry out, 'Abba! Father!' The Spirit Himself testifies with our spirit that we are children of God..." Romans 8:15-16.

Something Borrowed

God pardons like a mother,

who kisses the offense into everlasting forgiveness.

Henry Ward Beecher

Day 54 – Consider the Ravens

Perhaps your first thought upon hearing of the engagement was, "How will we pay for this?" Perhaps finances are not a stressful issue for your family. Either way, it does not hurt to ask God for guidance when it comes to wedding spending. Traditionally, your family would be expected to pay for the majority of ceremony and reception expenses. But perhaps your daughter and her betrothed are well-established financially and want to pay for things themselves. Maybe you have set aside a specific amount to contribute to the wedding, and you will let them make up the difference. The groom's parents may offer to cover some expenses which normally fall to the bride's parents. These days, there are thousands of scenarios for the who-pays-what puzzle in wedding planning. Pray now for clear communication, unity, and the resources to create a special day your family will remember forever.

Father, you know all about the finances involved in pulling off this event (Luke 12:22-31). My head is swirling with the costs of venue rental, clothing, food, gifts, musicians, photographers, flowers, and decorations—not to mention travel. My heart's desire is to provide my daughter with the wedding of her dreams. Give me a clear vision of how to do that in a way which promotes peace with all involved. Provide unity as my husband and I discuss our budget and resources. Give us an extra measure of understanding in any potential areas of conflict during the planning process. Please protect our income during this time and supply creative ways for us to cover expenses.

Help me not to be driven by my expectations but to allow the bride and groom to set the tone for expenditures. Please stifle any impulse to be miserly in such a once-in-a-lifetime situation. Help me to be generous and see a need before I am asked to provide for it. Give me honest humility to admit when I don't have the resources to give. Provide us all with great creativity in using the funds you provide to their fullest extent. Protect us from impulse spending and keep us out of debt.

Provide talented, honest, reasonably-priced vendors for the ceremony and reception. If there are contracts to be signed, give us the wisdom and realistic thinking to not entangle ourselves with poor legal decisions. As unforeseen expenses or income disruptions occur, provide solutions for each obstacle. Protect us from any problem which would deplete the resources needed to cover wedding costs. May the technical aspects of all payments go through without a hitch.

May there be no fear, bullying, hurt feelings, misunderstandings, or bitterness which arise from the wedding finances. Help my family and that of the groom to create a fair, clear plan agreeable to all. Thank you for providing, through your grace, for every need as we weave the tapestry which will be the beautiful celebration of my daughter's wedding. Amen.

Something Borrowed

Contentment, rosy, dimpled maid,

Thou brightest daughter of the sky.

Catherine Rebecca Grey (Lady Manners)

Day 53 – Above All Else

Although Jesus cares deeply about every detail of our lives and of the wedding process, never forget there is only one thing that truly matters when it comes to your daughter. Her relationship with Christ is the cornerstone, bottom line, starting point, and the sum total of every metaphor we can conjure having to do with foundations. If your daughter has a strong relationship with Christ, sing songs of praise for that today and pray that she will always cling to her savior. If her spiritual condition is not what you had hoped it would be, take time to ask God for mercy and change.

Father, we know from your word that you desire all to be saved (1 Timothy 2:4). I pray in your strong name today for my daughter and cry out for mercy on her soul. I claim her on the basis of the shed blood of Jesus and pray her heart would always turn to you in truth. Help my daughter to grasp that Jesus Christ lived and died so she might be able to enjoy God's presence fully here on earth and for an eternity hereafter. If she has never made a commitment to you, I pray she will not wait another day or another minute to seek forgiveness, to believe you died to give her life, and to begin living in unity with you.

Give my sweet daughter clarity of mind and spirit to consider and believe "...if you confess with your mouth Jesus as Lord, and believe in your heart that God raised Him from the dead, you will be saved; for with the heart a person believes, resulting in righteousness, and with the mouth he confesses, resulting in salvation. For the Scripture says, 'Whoever believes in Him will not be disappointed'" Romans 10:9-11.

Where I have failed to model or communicate the impact of your loving sacrifice on the cross, I repent. Thank you for covering my parenting errors with your patience and forgiveness. Give me the strength and vision to uproot any bitterness which creeps in as I consider where my daughter's father's spiritual parenting may have fallen short.

I beg for mercy on the soul of my future son-in-law as well. May he be a godly husband and father and a strongly positive spiritual influence on my daughter as they build their lives on earth. I boldly pray for any children they may have, that my grandchildren would not only know Jesus as savior, but also be used as tools to bring others into your kingdom.

Help them to be courageous witnesses to the world around them. Protect them from the assaults of the enemy as they forge ahead in the creation of a Christ-centered home and family. Bring them into a strong and healthy Christian fellowship that will encourage them to lead a life steeped in unity, prayer, evangelism, forgiveness, and kindness. Amen.

Something Borrowed

They shall speak of the glory of thy kingdom,

And talk of thy power;

To make known to the sons of men his mighty acts,

And the glory of the majesty of his kingdom.

Thy kingdom is an everlasting kingdom,

And thy dominion endureth throughout all
generations.

Psalm 145:11-13 (KJV)

Day 52 – A Cloud of Witnesses

What an honor for a young lady to be asked to serve as a bridesmaid. And what important decisions your daughter must make as she considers which of her friends and relatives to have by her side at the altar. Hopefully, her choice of bridesmaids is thrilling your heart because you know the group of young women will bring joy to your daughter as they dream together of her new life with her beau. However, you may be afraid she is choosing foolishly and inviting unnecessary drama to the wedding process. You may anticipate trouble with that unwitting friend who doesn't realize the time commitment, expenses, and other responsibilities the festivities will bring her way. Your daughter may even have chosen a maid of honor who is so chronically tardy you doubt she'll make it to her own wedding on time. Pray today for your daughter, her attendants, and all those who will play a key role as they celebrate the sacred vows before God.

Lord, today I pray for my daughter's bridesmaids. Be with her and her groom as they determine the size of the wedding party. Help them to be realistic and consider their budget and venue carefully before making any final choices. Create full agreement between them on all decisions regarding the wedding party.

Give my daughter wisdom as she considers which of her friends and relatives to ask to participate in such a special way. May they be women who choose to honor you in the pre- and post-wedding activities, who will encourage my daughter to be a godly wife, and will support her transition from single to married life. May there be no jealousy or negativity among the bridesmaids. If my daughter comes to me for guidance about her choices, give me wise words.

Otherwise, guard my mouth and help me keep opinions to myself. Remind me to bring my fears to you.

As the women are asked to participate, give each one wisdom about whether or not to accept. Help them to take honest stock of their time and finances, and give them the courage to decline if it is best. If any of them tend to be irresponsible, give them an extra measure of timeliness and efficiency during the wedding events.

I pray there will be no disappointment or hurt feelings if someone is not asked to participate. If there are strained friendships or family relationships in my daughter's life, use this as an opportunity for reconciliation and not furthering of dissention. May bitterness dissolve and forgiveness abound in this situation.

I also pray for my son-in-law-to-be as he chooses attendants. Give him wisdom and provide resources for each groomsman to participate fully. Reveal to me ways to lighten their loads.

May none of the attendants be a source of stress or negativity for the bride or groom during these days. Help each one to plan ahead and not overlook important details about their attire or responsibilities. Provide these men and women with everything they need and give them safe travel to and from the wedding. Fill them with your joy and peace and create an atmosphere where wonderful memories will be made. Amen.

Something Borrowed

Our friends interpret the world and ourselves to us,
if we take them tenderly and truly.

A. Bronson Alcott

Day 51 – There's No Place Like Home

One of many crucial choices your daughter will be making during this time is where she and her groom will live as they begin life as one. Will he move into her place, or she into his? Will they live with you for a time as they get their financial footing? Will they be making a long-distance trek for a new job or military assignment? Will they rent or buy? Are they asking for advice or keeping their thoughts to themselves? Although the choice of where to live is not as crucial as the choice of whom to marry, a poor decision can come with a high price. Pray for opportunities and discernment as the newlyweds sift through their options.

Father, as my daughter and her fiancé begin to explore where to live after the wedding, give them endless wisdom and clear thinking. As they discuss their desires and examine opportunities, give them unity and excellent communication. Help them to carefully consider the lifestyle they intend to lead during their first year of marriage and to plan realistically.

Open up the perfect living situation for them. Give them selections that are within their budget and spacious enough for their comfort. Provide a safe neighborhood and good neighbors. Give them a realistic picture of all the costs involved in their dwelling choice, such as utilities or commuting expenses. If they have any special needs such as a pet-friendly apartment, or space for a home office, please supply that as well.

Provide godly counselors who can guide them and help with budgeting decisions. Help me to keep opinions to myself unless asked to share them. Give me a heart of generosity if they will be living closer to the groom's family than to mine. May this not become an opportunity for jealousy to develop on either side of the aisle.

Help them to steer clear of any negative legal entanglements, unsafe or unhealthy dwellings, or hidden costs. Protect any deposits or escrow accounts. May they be exposed only to honest landlords, realtors, or mortgage brokers.

Provide safe and affordable options as they begin to move their belongings into their love nest. If the newlyweds must pare down furniture or other belongings, make that a peaceful process for them. If they are missing furniture or accessories in order to make the home comfortable, provide abundantly for that need.

Fill their home with love, joy, peace, and patience that only you can provide. May it be a place of harmony where their gifts of hospitality bloom and provide a sweet fragrance to all they know. In Jesus' name, amen.

Something Borrowed

A cottage will not hold the bulky furniture and sumptuous accommodations of a mansion; but if God be there, a cottage will hold as much happiness as might stock a palace.

Dr. James Hamilton

Day 50 – The Honor of Your Presence

Although it may be tempting to drop the invitation process into some lesser "administrative" category of wedding planning, don't be fooled. Those little pieces of paper are a capstone to the event, whether it be big or small, religious or secular, local or destination. No other single item has a greater potential to create misunderstandings, division, or hurt feelings. Who decides on the headcount? Which friends or family will make the cut? Who will pay for the printing and postage? Who will direct the laborious task of gathering addresses and putting the mailing together? Who will tally RSVPs (if you even bother with RSVPs)? The questions are endless, as are the scenarios which do not end well. Let's ask God to intervene today as we consider the guest list and invitation process.

Lord, I know that invitations hold special symbolic significance in Scripture. From Jethro's admonition to his daughters to invite Moses for a meal (Exodus 2:20), to the sacred invitation to the marriage supper of the lamb heard by John and recorded in Revelation 19:9, the call to join in meals and festivities rings through history. Thank you for your heart for celebrations and your abundant provision to share my daughter's wedding with friends and loved ones.

Please provide wisdom and generosity for all involved as we compile a list of those we would like to have in attendance. Give us ears to hear the wishes of the bride and groom and the good sense to honor those wishes. May no preconceived notions of any family members rob the couple of the wedding of their dreams. Put a guard around my mouth if their decisions threaten to disappoint me for any reason. Please give me diligence and energy to accurately organize the names and addresses of those I would like to invite.

As my daughter and her groom work on the design and content of the mailing, please provide unity and resources for them to create an invitation which reflects their special personalities. Provide reasonably priced designers and printers who operate with integrity, meet deadlines, and provide excellent customer service. May any research regarding maps, registries, and accommodations be accurately reproduced and distributed. May any electronic means of communicating with guests be easy to access and understand.

Before the printing is completed, give us the skill to proofread the invitations and all inserts carefully. May there be no wasted expense due to mistakes or typos. May there be no mistakes regarding postage, no lost or delayed mail, and no incorrect addresses. If the invitations are sent electronically, please allow them to be delivered without mishap.

As the RSVPs start to come back, or we begin tallying a headcount based on word-of- mouth, keep us organized and realistic about the number of guests to expect. May the estimate of attendees be accurate and not cause any shortage or overage regarding seating or catering.

If there are any discrepancies or hurt feelings regarding who received an invitation or who did not, please reveal that before bitterness can grow. Please pour out your spirit of peace on the hearts of any who are hurt by not being invited and do not allow them to feel unloved or unwanted. In your mighty and ordered name we pray, amen.

Something Borrowed

Nothing annoys people as much as not receiving invitations.

Oscar Wilde

Day 49 – Celebrate Good Times

Even in these modern times with roles thrown about willy-nilly, reception planning and funding usually fall under the purview of the bride and her family. And even in these modern times that means you, the mom, may find yourself the primary planner and organizer of the food and surrounding activities. If you haven't already begun to arrange the who, what, when, and where for that occasion, now is the time to get organized. If you put down a deposit with a caterer the week the engagement was announced, now is the time to put the finishing touches on the plans. Either way, today is the day to ask God's blessing on this gathering which will honor your daughter and her groom in a once-in-a-lifetime fashion.

I come to you today, Lord, with the reception in mind. I am so overwhelmed by the choices and responsibility and can't take another step without you! As my daughter and I work together, please provide the perfect solution to the puzzle of place, time, décor, and menu. May there be no confusion or problems with the reservations or location of the event. Give my husband and me unity of mind and spirit as we make plans. Help me communicate my expectations and to respect his desired level of involvement in the process and the event itself. Protect us from unexpected expenses or any financial liability due to contract misunderstandings or unscrupulous people. Provide financially for the meeting space, entertainment, and food, and give us insight in any ways we might be more frugal.

Lord, please give us the energy and time in these busy days to stay organized and on top of all the details of the reception. Help me to consider and discuss with my daughter and future son-in-law their desires for the evening. Give me great creativity to be able to honor them and celebrate their lives both as individuals and as a couple. Bring people across my path to assist with aspects of the evening I don't have a skill set to pull off. As I plan decorations, seating arrangements, menu choices, and even what to wear, keep the decision-making from stealing my peace.

If there are any technical aspects of the evening, such as special music or a slideshow, protect us from difficulties with equipment. Be with the attendants and parents or grandparents who will speak, and provide courage and the exact right words for them to say.

May the food preparers and servers be attentive and conscientious. May the food be delicious and to the liking of each guest. I beg your mercies for safe travel, and adequate directions and parking.

I ask that as we pray and celebrate as Christians throughout the evening, your name would be honored among the many people watching from the wings. Thank you for caring so tenderly about every detail. With heartfelt gratitude, amen.

Something Borrowed

"Let us rejoice and be glad and give the glory to Him, for the marriage of the Lamb has come and His bride has made herself ready." It was given to her to clothe herself in fine linen, bright and clean; for the fine linen is the righteous acts of the saints. Then he said to me, "Write, 'Blessed are those who are invited to the marriage supper of the Lamb.'"

Revelation 19:7-9a

Day 48 – Forever on Side by Side

Can you picture it? The good-byes have been said, the bubbles blown, and your daughter and her groom get in the car and begin to drive away. Pause and imagine the emotions coursing through you as they roll out of sight—closing the book on one chapter of your family's life, and opening another. After you take a minute to dry your eyes, let's pray today about the honeymoon. Whether they intend to travel to an exotic destination or trek to the closest campground, the memories they make during the once-in-a-lifetime trip will be priceless. Let's pray for God's hand of blessing and protection as they drive off into the sunset together as man and wife.

Heavenly Father, I can't even imagine what it will feel like in those moments when my baby girl begins her new life. I know she was never mine to begin with, she has always been yours, but it is such a stark reminder that things will never be the same. Comfort my heart as that time approaches, and give me strength to express sincere joy and gratitude for the chance to be her mom.

As the bride and groom are planning and preparing for the honeymoon, give them discernment regarding destination and timing. Provide unity in the decision-making and realistic financial planning regarding the potentially large expense. Bring opportunities for budget-friendly travel. Create a window of opportunity in work and school so they might have an extended time to celebrate the wedding and begin to build the marriage.

Work out every detail of the vacation—flights, rental cars, passports, immunizations—and give the couple diligence to be well-

prepared and avoid any last-minute panic situations. Give them clear thinking while packing, and provide for every need as they get organized. Grant them health as they travel and protect them from accidents or the intentions of evil people. Put your angels around them and bring them home safely. Comfort my heart and keep me from the temptation to worry while they are traveling.

If they are unable to arrange their ideal honeymoon at this time, create contentment in their hearts with the plans they can realistically arrange. Keep the dream of a romantic getaway alive for them to look forward to at another time.

Lord, I know that our ideas of the perfect vacation don't usually come to full fruition. If there are any disappointments for the sweet couple as they travel together, soothe them and create grace rather than discord in the circumstance. As they set out to explore physical, spiritual, and emotional oneness, bless them with a foundation of pure vulnerability that will carry them through the years.

Please provide a spirit of joy that begins on the trip and carries over into their new home when they return. Remind them each day of your love and draw them to you. In your blessed name we pray, amen.

Something Borrowed

Like an apple tree among the trees of the forest,

So is my beloved among the young men.

In his shade I took great delight and sat down,

And his fruit was sweet to my taste.

He has brought me to his banquet hall,

And his banner over me is love.

Song of Solomon 2:3-4

Day 47 – It's the Thought That Counts

Ribbons and cupcakes and gift bags—oh my! Here come the parties and showers to honor your daughter and her groom and provide a solid start for their home through the generous gifts of friends and family. Far from the old-fashioned ladies in dresses drinking tea, modern showers run the gamut of creative themes and may even include the groom and other male guests. As you look forward to these gatherings, there may be additional stress placed on you as you plan more travel, purchase special gifts, choose your wardrobe, and advise and encourage your daughter in her role. You might even be hosting a party yourself (which Emily Post says is now allowed). Whatever your circumstances, thank God today for another chance to celebrate.

Lord Jesus, I am so grateful for the opportunity my daughter and her fiancé have to be blessed physically with gifts. But beyond the provision of things, I thank you for their friends and family who choose to honor them and pour themselves into making these memories. Tuck these times away in my daughter's heart as special moments where she is the center of attention, and allow me to enjoy watching her sit as the belle of the ball.

As each shower is planned, grant the hosts abundant creativity and energy to make the event memorable. Give them wisdom in choosing a location, compiling a guest list, and planning the itinerary. Provide financially for the substantial costs of gifts, decorations, and food, and give each host the resources without incurring debt. Help me not to overlook any opportunities to be of service. Create a spirit of unity if there are multiple hosts, and please don't allow any hurt feelings or bitterness to arise because of disagreements or misunderstandings. I ask that there be no mishaps with the invitations and that all who wish to attend would feel loved and included. Please don't allow anyone to be overlooked. Alleviate any unrealistic expectations the hosts may place on themselves and allow true joy to be the theme of each party.

Please guard and protect guests as they come and go. May the location be clearly communicated and easy to access. Provide health and transportation for each one to attend. Give any without resources to purchase a gift a clear signal they are welcome to attend anyway. May no one be embarrassed about their gift-giving abilities.

As guests who don't know each other begin to gather together, may each one feel included and important. Please create an atmosphere of friendliness and love, and provide bold confidence as I mingle and get to know the groom's friends and family.

If there have been no shower plans made and time seems to be running out, give me wisdom regarding whether or not to initiate one myself. May the bride and groom feel especially treasured and celebrated during these next few weeks as we gather to extend our love and best wishes for their future. Amen.

Something Borrowed

The heart of the giver makes the gift dear and precious.

Martin Luther

Day 46 – Takin' Care of Business

Whether you work full-time in an office or part-time in a store, stay at home raising children or designing websites, volunteer at church or a nursing home, your days were full long before the wedding planning began. How will you possibly juggle work and the load these preparations are already adding to your day? Should you resign, or cut back your hours? Should you hire someone to clean your home? Should you ask your husband to do more around the house? The good news is that moms have been juggling work and wedding planning for centuries. Ask the Lord to keep your mind focused on him as you take on even more responsibility.

Lord Jesus, thank you for the work you have so generously supplied for me to do each week. Thank you for the opportunity to use the talents and gifts you have given, to provide physically for my family, and to serve my community.

As I am contemplating the time and distraction that wedding planning is adding to my workday, I beg you for help. Please give me a clear picture of the calendar and what I need to do when. Keep me organized, but also keep me from worry. If I need to set aside any responsibilities during this time, give me the courage to do so. Please fill in the gaps I will leave behind. Give me an extra measure of energy and protect me from accidents and illnesses which would use up precious hours.

Help my boss, co-workers, customers, or other children to be supportive and understanding during these next few weeks. Create an atmosphere of flexibility in all our schedules. Help me to see when a task can wait until after the wedding, but keep me from using it as an excuse for poor performance. Thank you for the special insight this will give me to come alongside any co-workers who will be planning a child's wedding in the future.

Please bring advisers and encouragers to help me stay balanced and focused. Reveal a truthful view of the vacation time I need to schedule both before and after the ceremony. If this time results in lost wages, give my family and me creative ways to make up the difference. Give my husband and me complete unity about any changes in hours or work status, and please, Lord, remind him to pick up his socks.

Help me to use this as an opportunity to step back and examine my daily routine. Use it as a time to improve productivity, eliminate time-wasting habits, and make my workday even better in the days following the wedding.

Continue to bring to my mind the fact that moms have been doing this for centuries. My stress is nothing new under the sun, and certainly nothing you can't handle. Thankful you are with me always, amen.

Something Borrowed

Therefore they said to Him, "What shall we do, so that we may work the works of God?" Jesus answered and said to them, "This is the work of God, that you believe in Him whom He has sent."

John 6:28-29

Day 45 – Heigh-Ho

Your daughter will likely spend more time working than participating in any other activity during her lifetime. She may dream of being a stay-at-home mother, but before and after those child-rearing years she will probably be a working woman. So whether she is still in school or solidly entrenched in a career, your prayer support will make an immeasurable difference in the quality of her life. Likewise, your future son-in-law's work and scholastic efforts will benefit from your prayers, especially if his own mother has not taken on that responsibility. Ask your children for specific ways you can support them spiritually in this area and then follow through with the great privilege of bringing their careers before God.

Lord, thank you for the ability my daughter has had to study and work, and the successes you have already provided. Thank you for good teachers and other caring adults who have helped her navigate the school years. If she is still unsure what the future holds for her career, bring along desires and opportunities in line with her talents and help her not to overlook an option you have for her. Help her to seek out and listen to wise counsel regarding her educational or career path.

While my daughter and her husband are in school, open doors for them at the best institutions. Provide wise and godly instructors who can help mold them during this formative time. Provide the financial resources, housing, and transportation they need to complete their studies. Send a spirit of diligence and discernment as they juggle school and marriage. Show me what I can do to encourage and support them.

Help my daughter to know without a doubt that her job does not define her. Teach her to draw her identity from you, as a child of the Most High God. If she chooses homemaking as a career, give her an extra measure of self-esteem when the world might question her value. If she is a working mother, provide trustworthy day care and an environment that is supportive of her role at home. Give her the great energy and creativity of the Proverbs 31 woman, with boldness to balance business and home management. Lavish her with the talent and skill required to excel at her job, but keep her from a prideful spirit when she does. Guard her from any temptation to participate in workplace relationships or activities that are not pleasing to you. Give her the wisdom to encourage and support her husband in his career.

I pray for my future son-in-law as well. May he draw his worth from you, Lord, and not from any activity or title he holds. Give him strength for the times he may be the sole provider for his family; may he keep his eyes fixed on you as the one who gives every blessing. Give him insights and energy to encourage and support my daughter in her career.

I pray that my daughter and her future husband would be blessed with great success in their jobs as noted by the wise poet: "Do you see a man skilled in his work? He will stand before kings; He will not stand before obscure men" Proverbs 22:29. Amen.

Something Borrowed

Unless a man works he cannot find out what he is able to do.

Philip Gilbert Hamerton

Day 44 – The Invisible Man (and Woman)

It's very unfortunate, but if someone with behind-the-scenes wedding day responsibility doesn't do his or her job, the focus quickly shifts from the happy couple to the unhappy attendees. When guests arrive to find a dirty restroom, or a thermostat that wasn't turned on in time to cool or heat the church, the memories made may not be as pleasant as you would hope. The last thing you need is a phone call from a venue manager complaining that the catering staff did not clean up their mess. What a shame it would be if the limousine driver hired as a special gift from Grandpa failed to show up on time to whisk the couple away. And let's face it—as the mother of the bride you will likely be the one pulled aside to solve the problem. Take time to pray today that every person who has even the smallest role in the wedding will do his or her job well.

Lord, what a complicated puzzle this event is turning out to be! I had no idea so many people would be required to pull it off. When I think about the diligent efforts that are going into making great memories, I am so thankful. Thank you for providing the talented, hardworking people who have agreed to help in so many ways. Keep me from worrying about each of them doing things the way I would like to have them done, and help them to complete their tasks without my interference.

I pray that every person who has a behind-the-scenes role to play in any part of the wedding will operate with the utmost conscientiousness. I pray for health and diligence for our wedding planner, ceremony and reception venue staff, food preparers, servers, transportation staff, custodians, florists, decorators, hair and makeup technicians, and the photographer's team. For family and friends who have volunteered for specific tasks, I ask that you give them an extra blessing for their loving generosity. Put your angels around them and get them where they need to be when they need to be there.

Please give each one (myself included) a spirit of honoring others before ourselves. Make us quick to help in ways that may not be in our specific job descriptions. Help us to see needs and take care of them quietly and without complaint (Philippians 2:14). Make your charitable spirit known through us when unforeseen problems arise.

Lord, I ask that any potential roadblocks would be revealed well in advance, and that suitable solutions would come to our minds. For those last-minute hiccups, I beg for mercy as we find resolutions. Protect my daughter and her groom from any knowledge of potentially upsetting behind-the-scenes issues they can't control.

Help me keep an eternal perspective about all the facets of this event which may not go the way they were planned. I know I can't direct every detail, but you have things well in hand. My desire is that you, Lord, be glorified in every way as the events unfold. Continue to use me to that end. In your name I pray, amen.

Something Borrowed

When we trust our brother, whom we have seen, we are learning to trust God, whom we have not seen.

James Freeman Clarke

Day 43 – Daisy, Daisy

Even the most minimalist bride and groom will likely want flowers included in their ceremony and reception. Whether you snag a talented friend to create silk arrangements in advance, snip blooms from someone's garden, or hire a florist to design elaborate bouquets and centerpieces, floral decorations bring a special beauty to the celebration. Let's pray today that the flowers and other ornamentation will not be a source of stress in any way, but rather a lovely dose of traditionalism which adds to the sweet memory of the day.

Father, thank you for the beauty of creation which we experience through flowers and greenery. What a wonder it is to feel the rush of pleasure at the colors and textures of flowers. I look forward to the beauty that flowers will bring to the wedding ceremony and reception, and the lovely bouquets and boutonnieres that will make each special participant feel honored.

Please give all the wedding planners a united spirit as discussions about the flowers and decorations begin. Let the bride's and groom's voices be heard loud and clear as they communicate their dreams and wishes with each other and with their families. Give them wisdom as they consider the participants' needs, venue layout, and even the seasonal advantages of different types of blooms.

If my daughter and her fiancé are hiring a florist, help them to plan well in advance so they have options to find just the right shop. Give the florist a gifted listening ear as they communicate their desires for the decorations. Help the florist to take excellent notes that will be easy for the shop staff to decipher when they set out to fill the order. *Give them a fair price, an honest florist, and provide financially for this expense. Let there be no surprise charges the day of the wedding. Keep the florists' paperwork organized and provide the stock of flowers and accessories they need the day they begin putting the order together. May any deliveries go flawlessly.*

If there is to be a less conventional approach to the flowers for the wedding day, give us creativity and the financial resources to make that happen. Provide a project manager who can coordinate the team needed to put the flowers and decorations together.

Help us to plan well for any other accessories such as candles, candelabras, pew bows, aisle runners, flower girl baskets, ring bearer pillows, photographs, centerpieces, directional signage, extra lighting, or ornamentation for the guest book, gift, or cake tables. Provide the creativity and people needed to carry off a lovely atmosphere in both the ceremony and reception. Please also bring together some joyful, energetic folks to clean it all up when the day is over.

When the time comes, please provide enough corsages and boutonnieres for all involved and let there be no hurt feelings if someone has been overlooked. May there be no mishaps with pins or allergies. May the expectations of my daughter and her groom be met and exceeded, especially with the bride's bouquet. Thank you for the joy the simple adornment from your bounty will provide during this special time. Amen.

Something Borrowed

Lovely flowers are smiles of God's goodness.

William Wilberforce

Day 42 – Just Relax

Even if you are one of those fortunate women who normally doesn't have trouble falling asleep at night, you may be finding yourself tossing and turning a little at this point in the wedding planning process. Just when your head hits the pillow, you begin second-guessing the day's activities. Memories of tasks undone, words unsaid, and plans unmade may threaten to keep you wide-eyed for hours. If you are a habitual worrier, this nighttime ritual may begin to spin completely out of control. Just think of all the other members of your family and family-to-be who might be having the same sleep issues. Thankfully, the Lord has provided the best solution to a lack of rest—coming to sit at his feet in prayer and meditation on his word.

Heavenly Father, thank you so much for the invitation to rest. I am in awe at the rhythm of relaxation you have woven into all creation, and particularly into our human spirits and bodies. Thank you for the physical comforts of my life which make it easy to get a good night's sleep. Thank you for every answer and every soothing thought provided when I have trouble drifting off.

For any unhealthy routines which I have allowed to rob me of sleep, please provide a solution and the strength to kick the habit. Remind me of your holy word tonight:

"In peace I will both lie down and sleep, for You alone, O Lord, make me to dwell in safety." Psalm 4:8

"It is vain for you to rise up early, to retire late, to eat the bread of painful labors; for He gives to His beloved even in his sleep." Psalm 127:2

"Thou wilt keep him in perfect peace, whose mind is stayed on thee: because he trusteth in thee." Isaiah 26:3 (KJV)

Help me not to neglect the Sabbath and your modeling of rest (Genesis 2:3). No matter how tempting it is to try and get one more activity in, one more chore done, or one more phone call made, give me the good judgment to take a break and focus on the eternal. Even if I have not set a tone for Sabbath rest while raising my daughter, give me the wisdom to do so during these days and after the wedding as well.

I pray also for my daughter and her sleeping patterns over the next few weeks. Don't let her believe the lie that she is invincible and that a lack of rest won't affect her. Provide clear thinking as she maps out her schedule, and allow ample time for sleep and relaxation. Please do not let her wear herself out to the point where sickness will have easy access to her body. Help her to turn over to you both the worrisome and the exhilarating thoughts bombarding her mind as the wedding approaches so she can sleep well at night.

For the groom and his family, I ask your blessing of refreshing sleep. Help my future son-in-law rely on you so that he may rest well, knowing all the details of the celebration and life transition are held tenderly in your hands.

For all participants and attendees, I ask that no trouble or sickness would result from a frenzied lack of sleep. Please grant us the peace and calmness which can come only from your spirit. May "the peace of God, which surpasses all comprehension" guard our "hearts and minds in Christ Jesus" (Philippians 4:7). Amen.

Something Borrowed

Take rest; a field that has rested gives a beautiful crop.

Ovid

Day 41 – An Excellent Wife

The adornments of the bride will soon be packed away, but the adornments of her character will grace your family's life for years to come. As your daughter works hard to prepare for her wedding day and her upcoming role as a wife, Scripture has some very specific admonitions and encouragements for her. Pray through these words of wisdom and instruction and ask the Lord to weave them into your daughter's character, and if you are married, into yours as well.

Father, please teach my daughter to be a loving wife, remembering the words of Christ in the Great Commandment (Matthew 22:37-40): "... 'You shall love the Lord your God with all your heart, and with all your soul, and with all your mind.' This is the great and foremost commandment. The second is like it, 'You shall love your neighbor as yourself.' On these two commandments depend the whole Law and the Prophets." Teach her how to love you, Lord, while loving her husband well. Make their home a beacon of love as they practice hospitality. Draw her heart to yours and fill it with grace and forgiveness as she navigates the path of marriage. Help her love her enemies and pray for those who mistreat her (Luke 6:28).

Please teach my daughter to respect her husband: "Nevertheless, each individual among you also is to love his own wife even as himself, and the wife must see to it that she respects her husband" Ephesians 5:33. This submission and subjection topic has been so twisted it is almost unrecognizable in our generation. Forgive me for the ways I have not demonstrated respect for my own husband. I pray my daughter may be able to focus on and act out the teaching in a way that will feed and strengthen her relationship with her husband. May she clearly recognize any disrespectful thoughts or words formed against her husband and surrender them to you. I pray her words and attitudes toward him will come from a heart of grace and truth. May her respect embolden him to become a loving, confident, successful man with the resources and energy to serve you, Lord.

Please teach my daughter to surrender the authority she has over her own body as Paul teaches in 1 Corinthians 7:3-4: "The marriage bed must be a place of mutuality—the husband seeking to satisfy his wife, the wife seeking to satisfy her husband. Marriage is not a place to 'stand up for your rights.' Marriage is a decision to serve the other, whether in bed or out. Abstaining from sex is permissible for a period of time if you both agree to it, and if it's for the purposes of prayer and fasting—but only for such times. Then come back together again" (The Message). Create a healthy physical relationship that is never used as a weapon or tool of manipulation. Show her clearly the harm that will come when she is tempted to withhold affection out of fear, anger, or selfishness. May these instructions never be taken out of context or be twisted to condone any sort of physical or emotional abuse. I pray the mystery of the coming together of husband and wife would be glorifying to you in my daughter's marriage (Ephesians 5:32).

In Christ's name and for his sake, amen.

Something Borrowed

Your adornment must not be merely external—
braiding the hair, and wearing gold jewelry, or putting on
dresses; but let it be the hidden person of the heart, with
the imperishable quality of a gentle and quiet spirit, which
is precious in the sight of God.

1 Peter 3:3-4

Day 40 – The Beat Goes On

Wedding music is as quintessential to the day as wedding cake. It also has the potential to be the most disastrous element of any wedding ceremony. Who hasn't been to a service where a beloved aunt tried (and failed) to play the wedding march on the pipe organ? Has anyone thought about securing a sound technician or renting a PA system if necessary? Is there a backup plan if the reception DJ gets sick? Some churches will not allow musical instruments, others will insist on pre-approval of any secular music. Pray today for wisdom as your children choose not only the songs, singers, instruments and instrumentalists, but what part each will play in their celebration.

Lord, please give my daughter and her fiancé complete unity on any decisions having to do with music. As music is such a highly personal subject, allow them great transparency as they discuss options. Help all their family members to respect their wishes. Provide creativity as they consider selections for both the ceremony and reception. If there are talented musicians who are special to them, help those people to be available and willing to participate. Provide all the musical resources needed for singers and instrumentalists. Give the musicians the desire and time to practice well and do their best.

If they are hiring musicians, bring talented and conscientious people across their path. Please supply the funds necessary and help them to come to an appropriate agreement for any charges in advance. Remind the person responsible for making the payment to complete that task on the wedding day. Lord, please make funds available for tips, if necessary, and help each participant to feel included and appreciated.

If the bride and groom decide on recorded music, please furnish the appropriate sound system so everyone can enjoy the musical selections. Provide a talented sound technician to operate the equipment. We ask for your mercy to avoid technical issues which would distract from or interrupt the ceremony. If there is to be music at the reception, I pray the band or DJ would come with a God-honoring playlist. If there is a special song or two that would be meaningful to my daughter and her daddy as they dance together, bring them to my mind.

Help us all to think thoroughly through every aspect of the music well in advance. Give us solutions to any problems which arise. May we reflect your loving attitude as we deal with any potentially negative issues.

Father, may you be pleased by any music associated with my daughter's wedding day. Our desire is to bring you glory in all things. Amen.

Something Borrowed

Music is a kind of inarticulate unfathomable speech, which leads us to the edge of the infinite, and lets us for moments gaze into that.

Thomas Carlyle

Day 39 – The Best Job in the World

Whether you are already blessed with grandchildren around your table, or your daughter's marriage will be the first opportunity you have to look forward to that joy, it's time today to pray for God's most precious miracles. As a grandmother, you have a unique privilege and sacred responsibility to storm heaven's gates on behalf of your grandchildren. Take a few minutes right now to bathe the next generation of your family in prayer. (If for some reason you know you will never be a grandmother, why not ask God for an opportunity to reach out and influence another family as a godly surrogate grandmother.)

Father, what an honor it is to pray for my grandchildren. My heart is so full at the thought I can hardly stand it.

First of all, Lord Jesus, I ask that my grandchildren will come to know and believe in you at a young age, and that their lives would be built on faith in you and your sacrifice for them. Give them a clear sense of who they are in heaven's eyes and your best plan for them. Create in each child such a deep love for you and your ways that nothing else will seem comfortable. Help me to be sensitive and available at each stage of their spiritual development. Where I haven't yet matured to solid spiritual food, work in my heart to make my "senses trained to discern good and evil" (Hebrews 5:14). Make me a good teacher and an even better role model.

Lord, I beg for your peace and protection over my grandchildren all the days of their lives. Save them from illness and disease and heal them quickly of any infirmity which comes. Put your angels around them day and night that they might not be harmed by accidents or live with fear or anxiety in their hearts. Defend them from the plans of the enemy and from people with evil intentions.

Give these sweet ones healthy relationships as they continue to grow into adulthood. Create an atmosphere in our family where great love and friendships can blossom. Bring the influence of godly friends into their lives at every stage. Even now prepare the path each one will take to his or her own wedding day, as you desire.

Prepare my daughter's heart to be a mother. Make her a woman who is patient and kind, and has her priorities straight when it comes to family life. May she never fall into the comparison trap, but look to you for affirmation and encouragement. Give her a desire to sit at your feet, Father, to learn your ways in order to teach her own children. Draw her close to you and help her to love you more each day. Please give my new son-in-law the wisdom to parent well. As they add children to their family, keep them close to one another through the busyness of life.

I pray that each of my grandchildren would be filled to overflowing with your spirit as you teach them to love you more all the days of their lives. With eager anticipation I pray, amen.

Something Borrowed

Nothing happens unless first a dream.

Carl Sandburg

Day 38 – Dress Up Time

Hopefully by now the bride has chosen her gown, and it may even be hanging safely in her closet. Of course that is the most crucial wardrobe element, but it is far from the only consideration when it comes to who is wearing what during the wedding celebrations. One of your tasks at this point is to make final decisions about what you will wear and to communicate the tone of your apparel with the groom's mother. Garments' style, color, fit, and price must all be considered not only for the ceremony, but also for parties, showers, and the rehearsal dinner. Visions of earrings and pumps may be dancing in your head as you drift off to sleep at night. Then there is your husband. Is his tux ordered or has a new suit been purchased in time to be tailored? Are your other children counting on you to help shop for their attire? You may even be called upon to assist an older family member in choosing special occasion wear. Pray today for an eternal perspective on the external as final choices in attire are made over the next weeks.

Lord, I confess any anxiety about clothing to you right now. I don't know how such a relatively silly thing can grow into such a mountain of worry, but sometimes it does. I know from your word that I am not to fret about clothing, for you know exactly what I need. Give me wisdom to seek your kingdom and your righteousness first, knowing you will provide everything in your time (Matthew 6:32-33).

Keep my thoughts from being distracted by the myriad choices of clothing for my family and me. Provide outfits that honor you in style, fit, and cost. If items must be ordered or tailored, allow ample time for that to happen. Provide skilled tailors and seamstresses. May there be no confusion or mishaps with our garments. Give us all clear thinking about what we will need for each aspect of the celebrations, down to proper footwear for the venue. If we are traveling, bless us with clarity as we pack so there are no last-minute panic situations regarding clothing. Provide the finances needed for our wardrobes and keep us from debt.

I pray specifically that my daughter will make wise and timely clothing choices. May she and her groom be in agreement over colors, styles, and cost as they coordinate attire for the ceremony and other wedding celebrations. As they enter this most precious time of their lives as the center of attention, help them both feel attractive and adored, no matter what they wear.

I know that without the loveliness of your spirit on my face, no shiny jewelry or colorful dress will make any difference. My desire is for Jesus to be the reflection people see when any of my family members or I walk into a room. Fill us with the beauty of your holiness. Amen.

Something Borrowed

Is beauty vain because it will fade?

Then are earth's green robe and heaven's light vain.

John Pierpont

Day 37 – In the Pressure Cooker

Even the most well-matched, even-tempered couples will experience extreme stress from time to time during their engagement. Unfortunately, the tendency is often to become so focused on the upcoming event that they begin to neglect their relationship with each other. As the bride and groom generate and react to tensions over the coming weeks, ask God to have mercy on their hearts and minds, filling them with his spirit. The Apostle Paul tells us in Ephesians 6:10-18 that God's own armor is available for us to fight against spiritual forces which threaten our relationships with him and with each other. Pray today that your daughter and future son-in-law will put on the full armor, so they may move seamlessly and with joy into their lifetime commitment to each other.

Lord, today I pray for my daughter and her fiancé in your powerful name, claiming the tools for battle you have so generously provided. Give them knowledge and insight into the war being waged against them as Christians in this world. Keep them from fear, but help them to access these divine gifts promised to those who believe.

Belt of truth: Help my daughter and her future husband to recognize and denounce any deceptions the enemy brings into their thoughts or hearts. Allow them to live freely in honest communion with you and with each other. May the light of your word and spirit drive the darkness of delusion far from them, freeing them to soar as they move through their engagement and into a new life together.

Breastplate of righteousness: Lord, I cry out to you to release your righteousness in their lives! Make it their desire to know your word and align themselves to its purpose. May their hearts be quick to confess and release anything that is not pleasing to you, bringing unity to their pre- and post-wedding relationship.

Shoes of the gospel of peace: Lord Jesus, thank you that through you we have peace with God. I pray that my daughter and her fiancé would stay focused on you as they encounter potentially peace-robbing situations over the coming weeks. Give them your perfect peace as they trust you to light their paths for each step of the engagement process.

Shield of faith: May my daughter and her groom operate from a place of great faith, both now and in the future. Teach them to wield your holy shield well as they deflect the evil schemes of the enemy. Create in them a desire to step out boldly as you lead, and reward them "far more abundantly beyond all that we ask or think, according to the power that works within us" Ephesians 3:20.

Helmet of salvation: Father, may my daughter and future son-in-law both be assured of their place in your kingdom. If they have not received your forgiveness and taken on the helmet of our promised deliverance, I pray for their souls. If they have, lead them to put on the protection and identification you have so generously provided. May their every thought and action be pleasing to you.

Sword of the spirit: Lord, I ask you to create an unquenchable desire in my daughter's marriage for your holy word. May both of these precious ones crave time in study and prayer and allow it to drive every moment of their lives together.

Above all, I ask you to draw them to "pray at all times in the Spirit" (v. 16), bringing every petition to you with praise and thanksgiving. In the mighty name of Jesus, amen.

Something Borrowed

Onward, Christian soldiers, marching as to war,

With the cross of Jesus going on before!

Christ, the royal Master, leads against the foe;

Forward into battle, see his banner go!

Onward, Christian soldiers, marching as to war,

With the cross of Jesus going on before!

Onward, Christian Soldiers, Sabine Baring-Gould

Day 36 – Set Another Place

Has it really dawned on you yet? You are adding another member to your family: another seat around the table, another Christmas stocking, another birthday party to celebrate, and another soul to encourage, mentor, and love. What a precious time this is as your future son-in-law begins to contribute splashes of his spirit's color to the masterpiece of your family. Pray today for your daughter's husband-to-be, and ask the Lord to pour out his generous blessings on him as she moves through these next few weeks into the great adventure of marriage.

Heavenly Father, thank you for the privilege and joy it is to welcome a new son to the family. Thank you for bringing him across my daughter's path at just the right time so they might start a new life together as husband and wife. I praise you for the joy he has already brought into our home and for the wonderful times you have in store for our future together.

May this precious man daily choose to live according to your word and follow your ways. Help him to love you more and more as he grows in faith and service. Make him a student of your word, and give him a boundless desire to grow closer to you. Bless him with the encouragement and joy which come from Christian friendships. Help him to be a steadfast friend.

Jesus, I ask that this man's love for my daughter never stop increasing. Fill their home with affection and make it a place where short accounts are kept. When problems arise, provide wise counsel and give him godly solutions. May there be no divorce in their future.

Bless this young man with health, stamina, and resilience today and every day. Help him lead well at home and at work. Protect him from accidents, sickness and disease, and evil of any sort. Provide for his every need, physically, emotionally, and spiritually. May his heart embrace both the poor in spirit and the poor in goods.

If and when the time comes, please provide him with the desire, skills, and resources to be a wonderful father. Help him to be a sweet support to my daughter during pregnancy and childbirth. Give him great parenting wisdom from your spirit and your word. Keep his identity anchored in you and fill him with energy as the little faces clamor for love and attention. Keep the marriage strong throughout the years their children are growing.

Father, I pray a wonderful friendship and camaraderie would develop between my new son and me. Help us to establish a bond which is honest, open, and overflowing with grace. It is my desire to be a loving and supportive mother-in-law. Please provide the strength and discernment I need to relinquish my place on my daughter's priority list, and to establish healthy boundaries with the newlyweds. Open my heart wide to welcome the great blessing of a son-in-law and to begin a lifelong relationship of love and respect. Amen.

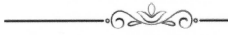

Something Borrowed

For there is no greater invitation to love,

than loving first...

St. Augustine of Hippo

Day 35 – Good Advice

Don't forget for one second that no matter how much stress you are under right now, your daughter is dealing with infinitely more. As the final days before the ceremony tick by, she is feeling the weight of responsibility for arguably the most important life decision she will ever make. Like you, she is also dealing with the frantic wedding prep activities on top of her already full schedule. Even if she is marrying the love of her life under the most ideal circumstances, she will no doubt be able to use a listening ear, and maybe even a shoulder to cry on, during these next weeks. Prepare your heart to cement your relationship and create a path of open communication while you march toward her wedding day together.

Father, I thank you for the privilege of being a mother to this young woman. Thank you for the time we have spent as mother and daughter, playing, praying, learning, and growing together. Thank you for the time we have now to dream and plan the bright future before both of us as she brings a new soul into our family. Lord, help these last days before the wedding be a time we can draw closer together and ensure our relationship is healthy as our new roles begin to take shape.

As she is knee-deep in decision-making, give me wisdom to offer guidance and advice when called upon. Help me to keep opinions to myself when not called upon. Help us both to learn well that the wants and needs of her groom come before my opinions and desires. Help me encourage her to be his cheerleader and biggest fan. May there be no misunderstandings or disagreements caused by my inability to step back and let my new son-in-law take his place in her life.

I love it when my daughter comes to me for advice, but I pray that she will always first turn to prayer and your word for comfort and wisdom. I pray she will trust in you, Lord, and not depend on her own understanding (Proverbs 3:5), that she will turn to wise counselors and not listen to foolish talk (Proverbs 13:20), and that she will honor her father and me, so she may have a long and successful life (Deuteronomy 5:16).

Forgive me for the times I have failed as a parent. Bring to my mind anything I need to confess to you right now. Bring to my mind anything for which I need to ask my daughter's forgiveness. Bring to my mind any hurts she may have caused me and give me the gift of forgiveness. Heal our relationship and prepare her to leave her father and me, and cleave to her husband (Genesis 2:24).

No matter how busy things get, keep my heart and schedule open and available for my daughter. Although she may never realize the depths of my love for her, Lord, you do, and you understand and love her even more than I do. Thank you for drawing us closer during this precious season of celebration. Amen.

Something Borrowed

A mother's prayers, silent and gentle,

can never miss the road to the throne of all bounty.

Henry Ward Beecher

Day 34 – Marriage Is Made in Heaven

The uniting of two people for a lifetime is a mystery as old as humankind itself. Civilizations, countries, neighborhoods, and families rest on a foundation of commitment between a man and woman to love and cherish each other for as long as they live. The symbolism of Christ's devotion to his bride, the church, is an enigma no one will fully grasp until we join him at the heavenly marriage supper (Revelation 19:9). In addition, the making of vows is no small thing. We see in Scripture many instances of people speaking rashly before God and paying exorbitant prices for their foolishness. We also see times where God is pleased with the making and keeping of vows. Let's shift our focus today from the wedding to the marriage itself. Pray for your own marriage as well as your daughter's as these daily reminders of your commitment to your husband motivate you to draw closer to God and ponder the beauty of your union.

Lord Jesus, thank you for the beauty of your love for the church which inspires and teaches us in our own marriages. Thank you that your commitment to us has no limits. I pray that our devotion to you will follow that example. Compel me to live as you did, with compassion and forgiveness, both in my marriage and in all my other relationships.

As my daughter and her groom state their marriage vows before you, speak clearly to their hearts about the sacredness of their words. Help them to weigh carefully the irrevocable nature of the promises they are making with the binding together of more than just their bodies. As they choose the words to say during the wedding ceremony, give them a picture of your desire for their time on earth as husband and wife. Create a sense of wonder at the ancient, magnificent, world-changing power of the pledges they are making. I ask that you will render their marriage a reflection of your love for the church, and that the beauty of their example will draw others to be reconciled with you.

I pray that my daughter will always find complete satisfaction in her marriage (Proverbs 5:19), and that the marriage bed will be held in highest esteem so she may not be judged (Hebrews 13:4). I pray against any inappropriate relationships or entertainment which may threaten the intimacy between my daughter and her groom. Protect them from the intentions of evil or misguided people. Protect them from the lies of the enemy, the selfishness of human nature, and any circumstances even tinged by the temptation of adultery. May there be no emotional or physical adultery in their future. Give them the creativity and desire to build a strong foundation of prayer, communication, friendship, forgiveness, physical intimacy, and vulnerability that will last through the blissful times and the storms to come.

Father, I echo your hatred of divorce (Malachi 2:16) and pray that my family and I will guard our spirits against dealing "treacherously" with our spouses. Our culture is so saturated with the filth of lust, self-indulgence, and betrayal. Lord, have mercy on us! Capture our thoughts and the intentions of our hearts and keep us focused on you as we purposefully and joyfully keep our marriage vows.

"What therefore God has joined together, let no man separate" (Matthew 19:6b). Amen.

Something Borrowed

What greater thing is there for two human souls than to feel that they are joined for life—to strengthen each other in all labour, to rest on each other in all sorrow, to minister to each other in all pain, to be one with each other in silent, unspeakable memories at the moment of the last parting.

George Eliot

Day 33 – A Fresh Grief

There really is nothing sweeter to a mama than having everyone she loves all in one place. Listening to the hum of familiar voices and reveling in the connection shared by family and close friends are some of the best moments of life. But what if there is a voice missing? What if a treasured soul isn't there to make memories and share in the excitement? Perhaps a beloved parent or grandparent has died prematurely, or perhaps there is estrangement within the family. Maybe disease or another hardship is forcing a loved one to miss these once-in-a-lifetime hours. How do we fill the gaping hole left because a special person's place is vacant? Let's ask God to help us grieve and to fill that hole as only he can. If you are so fortunate as to have each of your dear ones with you during this time, pray for other mothers who carry this additional burden on their child's wedding day.

Father, my heart is breaking at the thought of the next weeks and the wedding day going forward without my missing loved one. For so long, every picture I had in my mind of my daughter's wedding included this precious person. The pain is so intense sometimes I don't know if I can go on. Thank you for the assurance that those who have died with the hope of eternal life through Jesus Christ are waiting for us to join them in worship and celebration before the throne of heaven.

I know you hate death and estrangement, Lord, and that they were not part of your plan for humanity. I know you grieve when disease, anger, and evil of all sorts ruin dreams and relationships. If there is anything I can do to encourage healing in my family, prompt my spirit to obey and give me sound solutions. If there is division caused by my behavior, give me the strength to be humble and seek reconciliation. Thank you for the opportunity to bring good from this negative situation.

I know that you love me with a father's love, you are for me, and you will provide every strength and encouragement I need to get through this with grace. Help me to process the sorrow in a healthy way, and not to use disappointment as an excuse for ugly attitudes or words. Make me an example for other family members as I search your word and your face for comfort and courage in my sadness. Help me to remember others are grieving as well. Turn my heartache around and use it as a tool to draw them closer to you.

I affirm with the Apostle Paul that you are good, Lord, and I claim your peace for my family today: "Blessed be the God and Father of our Lord Jesus Christ, the Father of mercies and God of all comfort, who comforts us in all our affliction so that we will be able to comfort those who are in any affliction with the comfort with which we ourselves are comforted by God" 2 Corinthians 1:3-4. Amen.

Something Borrowed

You have taken account of my wanderings;

Put my tears in Your bottle.

Are they not in Your book?

Psalm 56:8

Day 32 – Blending In

It is said that you don't marry a person, you marry a family. Whether your daughter is going into a traditional first marriage or joining forces with a single father, issues of unity as their families begin to merge are never beyond the need for prayer. New parental, sibling, and extended family relationships loom before them with the potential for both joy and heartache. Ask God to continue to funnel all the positivity associated with the wedding day into future times when conflicts may arise.

Lord, as you look down on all the puzzle pieces that are our family, I beg for your mercy as things are shifting and changing with this momentous event.

For my daughter, I ask for an open heart to receive all the love her new relatives have ready to pour into her. If she is entering a challenging family situation, draw her close to you and give her abundant patience and wisdom in dealing with others. May her groom have the delight of seeing his wife fully love and accept his family of origin, and they her.

For my other children, I ask for excellent relationships with the new brother-in-law and his family. Give them all patient kindness and understanding as unmet expectations arise or misunderstandings threaten. Create an environment of clear communication for all my children. Help them to fully accept their new brother without hesitation.

For my husband and myself, I ask for great love and friendship to develop between us and our daughter's new in-laws. May we enjoy each other's company as we move into sharing life and co-grandparenting. May no jealousy or bitterness be allowed to develop at any time. May no critical words or thoughts of mine influence my daughter's relationship with her in-laws. May we clearly communicate love and acceptance of our new son-in-law.

For my extended family and that of the groom, I ask for open hearts and arms to welcome the new couple with unconditional love.

If my daughter or future son-in-law brings children or an ex-spouse into the mix, give everyone involved the love and patience supplied by the Holy Spirit to create a peaceful and healthy environment.

Lord, no matter how traditional or how complicated our new family situation is, thank you for knowing every detail. Control our hearts and minds as we move forward into the wonderful future you have for us all. Amen.

Something Borrowed

...walk in a manner worthy of the calling with which
you have been called, with all humility and gentleness,
with patience, showing tolerance for one another in love,
being diligent to preserve the unity of the Spirit in the
bond of peace.

Ephesians 4:1-3

Day 31 – Just Picture It

There are not many physical facets of the wedding celebration more important than the photography. Whether the bride and groom have hired a high-dollar audiovisual team, or they are counting on a friend to bring a nice camera and shoot some candids, the pictures will be irreplaceable treasures. Such a highly-charged job also has the potential for tragic mishaps and mistakes. Let's pray for the photographers and ask God to bless them as they capture the spirit of the day for us to enjoy in the years to come.

Lord, thank you for the resources we have to record this event with such clarity. Thank you for the memories we will be able to relish and the joy it will bring to our hearts to look back on the wedding and reminisce together.

If the bride and groom have hired a photographer, I pray they were able to find a talented and dependable professional, and made wise choices. I pray the cost is within their budget, and fees have been honestly and clearly communicated. May the photographers who come to record the festivities feel welcome and appreciated as they navigate the event. Provide health, safe travel, and clear directions as they come to the venue(s). We beg that they are not hampered by technical difficulties and that they are prepared with backup plans for any equipment failure. May the photos be edited and returned in a timely fashion. Guard the photographer's computer equipment and help them to store the photos wisely. Give them great skill and creativity as they shoot and edit the photos.

As we gather family units together, please give us clarity of mind to get all the group shots we need. If there are awkward family relationships, please provide grace for all interactions and do not give the enemy a chance to disrupt the peaceful tone of this day. If the bridal party or family will be traveling to different locations for photos, provide accurate driving directions and safe travel.

For the multitude of personal candid shots, I ask that you capture the joy of the day and the special personalities of those we love. Help us to gather and organize those shots well.

May the bride and groom's expectations of the pictures be met and exceeded. Lord, please come before any potential misuse of social media or distractions caused by personal photography.

As with all aspects of the wedding, may the photography honor you and your church as we strive to record the joy on our faces and in our hearts. Amen.

Something Borrowed

There are moments of life that we never forget.

Which brighten, and brighten, as time steals away;

They give a new charm to the happiest lot,

And they shine on the gloom of the loneliest day.

J. G. Percival

Day 30 – Take a Deep Breath

This is it! One month until the big day arrives, ready or not. Don't fall into the trap of believing your stressful striving over the next four weeks will make or break the event. Think of it like an airplane flight. You buy a ticket, plan and pack, but the plane will take off at (or near) the appointed hour whether you feel ready or not. Let that soothe the tendency to succumb to panicky thoughts about your to-do list. If there are a few things on the list that are never crossed off, the day will still be wonderful. If the bride and groom, officiant, and two witnesses show up, that is all that really must happen. Today, let's ask the Lord to provide an eternal perspective on the event, offering thanks for all he has done already, and trusting him to provide abundantly for every need that arises during this final month.

Jehovah-Jireh, God my provider, thank you for all you have done for my family and me since this wedding process began. Thank you for continued reminders that we are precious to you. Thank you for the privilege of bringing our hopes, fears, and jumbled thoughts on every topic to you as you patiently calm and counsel our souls.

As this final stretch looms ahead, I beg for mercy on my mind and emotions. Give me uncluttered thinking and abundant energy to perform the tasks ahead. Keep me from the temptation to err on the side of self-reliance and pride, or on the other hand, to shut down in panic while contemplating projects and timelines. Guard my mind and my mouth from any tendencies to criticize others in the way they handle their tasks and responsibilities.

For all who are participating in the nuptial events, I pray for abundant provision in terms of health, availability, finances, creativity, and peace during their preparations.

I pray for my daughter during this final period of her singleness. Keep me aware of her emotional state and in tune with her need for conversation, advice, or even just a hug. May she take time from the frenzy to reflect on her life and the goodness from your hand. If there is anything she needs to bring into subjection to your will, give her the wisdom and strength to submit. Remove any fear that may be creeping in regarding the great responsibility she is about to take on, and put in its place your love and strength. Provide her with insights and energy to be a devoted, godly fiancée to her groom during these days. Create sweet memories for them to cherish as the time of their marriage draws near.

For all the family members on both sides who will be eternally impacted by the wedding and also the marriage, I pray for peace as we anticipate a seismic shift in our worlds.

Thank you for the promise from the pen of the prophet: "Thou wilt keep him in perfect peace, whose mind is stayed on thee: because he trusteth in thee" Isaiah 26:3 (KJV).

Relying on you in all things, amen.

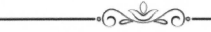

Something Borrowed

When peace, like a river, attendeth my way,

When sorrows like sea billows roll;

Whatever my lot, Thou hast taught me to say

It is well, it is well, with my soul.

It Is Well with My Soul, Horatio G. Spafford

Day 29 – Great Expectations

Be honest now—are your daughter's wedding plans coming together the way you have always envisioned them? Have you wished for her to wear your heirloom gown, or use your grandmother's engagement ring, or walk down the aisle in the church where she was raised? Odds are that most of your visions have evaporated as she and her groom plot and plan for their day. It is, after all, their day.

On the other hand, how many of your daughter's own engagement and wedding desires are not going to be fulfilled? Is her wish of an exotic beachside ceremony not financially feasible? Perhaps her fiancé is so painfully introverted that she is keeping the guest list small as a caring kindness to him. A wise woman will let the smoke of the vanishing dream clear without fanfare or bitterness, and move onto the beautiful reality before her. Today, ask the Lord to strengthen you and your daughter to let go of expectations and be thankful for blessings in any form.

Father, thank you for every good thing we have received from your hand as we plan and anticipate my daughter's wedding day. Forgive us for any griping or complaining we have allowed when things haven't worked out the way we had initially pictured them. Thank you for always supplying good solutions as we continue to piece this sacred event together.

Thank you for the sweetness of the dreams which have percolated in my mind over the years regarding what my daughter's wedding might be like. Thank you for the delightful times of make-believe with Teddy Bear grooms and hankie veils. Thank you for guarding her and guiding her to this time in her life. Thank you for the assurance of a future and hope during the hard days. Now that the future is here, guide me as I quietly lay down many of these visions in exchange for realistic circumstances. Keep me from the temptation to complain about the ideas of mine she is rejecting, or the things which are just impossible from a financial or logistical standpoint. Put in their place your perfect plan for these fleeting hours of preparation, and for the wedding day itself.

Lord, I may remember certain aspects of my own wedding day which were a great disappointment. Please forgive any bitterness or grudges I have held all these years regarding the things which did not go right. Move me beyond immaturity and help me recognize just how unimportant these issues really were. Give me an opportunity to share these memories with my daughter as an encouragement if it would help her process her own frustrations.

Please give my daughter the good judgment and courage to let go of any unreasonable expectations. Of course I want her to have the wedding of her dreams, but where she has an opportunity to consider another more important than herself (Philippians 2:3) give her the grace to do so. If there are insurmountable financial barriers to the dream wedding, help her to focus on the eternal aspects of the celebration—the people, the vow she is taking, and the mysterious bond she is entering into with the man she loves. Give us both a spirit of flexibility and grace to process any disappointments and to point others to your peace which "surpasses all comprehension" (Philippians 4:7).

In the strong name of Jesus Christ, amen.

Something Borrowed

Our brightest blazes of gladness are commonly kindled
by unexpected sparks.

Dr. Samuel Johnson

Day 28 - Serious Business

It is quite unfortunate how our culture has zeroed in on all the unpleasant aspects of in-law relationships. Just turn on the TV or pick up a joke book and you'll see and hear a plethora of negativity surrounding extended family relations. If these quips are to be believed, all mothers-in-law are condescending and all daughters-in-law unreasonable. Even if it is generally a true reflection of reality, it doesn't have to be that way for your daughter and her new parents-in-law. Pray today that she will strive to be an excellent daughter-in-law and to love her husband's parents unconditionally. Pray that they will accept and cherish her as they begin walking through the days ahead as a new family unit. This is no laughing matter, but rather as serious as it gets in terms of a healthy family legacy for generations to come. Pray hard.

Lord, why do these in-law relationships tend to be so complicated and fraught with turmoil? Of course it makes sense that it is ridiculously difficult to seamlessly add a member to a family, but I know through your strength and wisdom it is possible. Hear my prayer for my daughter as she begins forging a lifetime of bonds with her husband's parents.

I pray that you will give my daughter sensitivity to the difficult task her new in-laws have as they watch their son move out from under their wings. As responsibilities and expectations shift, keep clear lines of communication open between parents and children, and come before any conflicts with good solutions. Make my daughter sensitive also to any concerns her groom is feeling about his changing role in his family.

Please derail the potential for disrespect, suspicion, anger, and disappointment, and keep these negative emotions from ever making an appearance in their family. May no division occur due to misunderstandings, unmet expectations, or harsh words. May any conflict be dealt with quickly and decisively. Give them the desire to put others' needs first and live with Christlike servants' hearts before you (Philippians 2:3-7).

May the training my daughter has gained from me in how to be a good daughter-in-law serve her well. May she take the helpful things from the example set and leave behind the rest. Forgive my husband and me for times we have not established a positive tone with our in-laws, and give us the opportunity to make those mistakes right. Reveal to me any time my expectations or requests might cause conflict with my daughter's in-laws; I beg for enhanced sensitivity in this area.

I pray that my daughter will honor her husband's parents (even if it is sometimes difficult) and encourage him to do so as well, and that you may give them long life as they follow your will in this area (Exodus 20:12). May their healthy relationships serve as a beacon of positivity and a testament to the power of following your holy directives of love and respect. Amen.

Something Borrowed

God plans all perfect combinations.

David Brainerd

Day 27 – Child's Play

Oddly enough, many of the strongest opinions formed about the wedding day have to do with children. Some think a three-year-old is mature enough to be trusted as a centerpiece of a formal ceremony, and some don't. Some deem it proper to invite only the adults in a family when seating is limited, and some don't. Some believe the bride's or groom's children from previous relationships should be included in the wedding party, and some don't. Many prefer that children be excluded from the guest list due to their tendency to create a ruckus when least expected. Whatever the plans are for involving children in your daughter's wedding, ask God to make the little ones a source of delight and not a flashpoint for conflict or chaos.

Lord, thank you for the joy of children. I just love how they instinctively understand the sacred nature of weddings and your heart for celebrating. I pray that your will be done in regards to the children in our lives and this wedding event.

As the attendant and guest lists are considered, please allow the wishes of the bride and groom to be heard clearly and honored by other collaborators. If they choose to include special children in the ceremony, may those little ones be available to participate. May there be no conflict or jealousy among friends or family members regarding the couple's choices. Please provide the resources for them to be able to attend and not be a financial burden to their parents. Prompt me if there is any way I can help in this area.

If children are not to be included in the ceremony, silence the voices of those who are disappointed with that decision. If children are not to be included on the guest list, please allow the invitations to be received with grace and understanding. May these decisions not be a source of conflict with any friends or family members.

As we gather on the wedding day, please provide health, rest, refreshments, and diversions for the children. May their parents and caregivers have everything they need to attend to them during the marathon of photo, ceremony, and reception activities. Keep the children from any physical harm as the crowd of grown-ups will tend to be distracted with so many other things. Provide trustworthy adults to supervise the children if their parents are participating in the ceremony. Give the kids courage to walk the aisle and the self-control to move aside after carrying out their roles. I pray their tiny outfits and smiles will light the room with a special radiance as we celebrate.

May the memories created by the children live on vividly in their minds and ours as a sweet part of our family's history. Amen.

Something Borrowed

Blessed be childhood, which brings down something of
heaven into the midst of our rough earthliness.

Henri Frederic Amiel

Day 26 – A Possible Postlude

This may not even be on your radar, but have you considered what you will do the day after the wedding? Depending on your situation, this can be a sweet time to actually relax and enjoy any out-of-town guests, or even hang out with your daughter's new in-laws. Adrenaline will still be coursing, but not at a feverish pitch, and everyone will enjoy talking about the wedding and speculating on the fun the honeymooners are having. You and your husband may actually have time to look each other in the eye and speak in complete sentences once again! Ask the Lord to give you creativity and energy to plan one more special occasion in the wake of the wedding day festivities.

Lord, can I really even think about one more thing? If it is your timing and will that my family and I should get together following the wedding day, I rely on you to give me the desire to organize another party, as well as the creativity to pull it off in a special way. If we decide to go ahead with a post-wedding gathering, give my husband and me complete unity on all aspects of the planning. If we decide it is not best to schedule anything, give us peace and keep us from second-guessing the decision.

Help us to be realistic about the physical and emotional resources our family will have available at that time. The last thing we want to do is create more expectations that are not possible to fulfill when we are drained in every way. Give us clear thinking when making the guest list, and keep this from being an opportunity for hurt feelings. Help anyone who feels they don't have the ability to attend to not feel obligated. Keep me organized and on top of any last-

minute details regarding the meeting place, food preparation, or contacting guests.

When the time comes, give us the humility to say "yes" to anyone who asks if they can help. If it is at our home, please help us stay motivated to clean and cook as much as possible in advance. If it is at another place, please provide clear communication with our guests and the venue regarding times, directions, and menu choices.

When we gather, Lord, create an atmosphere of love and excitement and derail any tendencies toward complaining about things which may not have gone well during the wedding or reception. May we celebrate our family unity and just have fun together. Be with us in that place and fill us with your spirit of joy as we reminisce about the wedding and relish the beautiful snapshot of our family in this moment in time. With a heart full of gratitude and delight, amen.

Something Borrowed

There is an emanation from the heart in genuine hospitality which cannot be described, but is immediately felt and puts the stranger at once at his ease.

Washington Irving

Day 25 – We Are Family

As these final days before the wedding fly by, have you thought about how all the hubbub is affecting the bride's siblings? You remember them, right? Your other children? Their world is being shaken nearly to the same extent as yours: sharing their sister, helping her pack and move, watching as her time is taken up by another family, adjusting to a new normal. They likely have lots of emotions to process. Who better to help them do that than you, with the help of your heavenly Father? Take time today to ask the Lord how to best love your other children when the focus is unmistakably on their sister. If your daughter is an only child, pray today for any siblings she will gain when she becomes a sister-in-law.

Father God, for these children I prayed, and you heard my voice and answered me (1 Samuel 1:27). Thank you for the privilege of being a mother. Thank you for entrusting these lives to me as I was surely unfit to take on the task without you. Thank you for the dangers you have protected them from as they have grown and begun to explore the world. Thank you for the laughter that has rung through our house in the past years, for the tears I was able to wipe away, and for the love which continues to grow. Thank you for the joys you have provided even in the dark times when things were not easy.

Lord, I have made so many mistakes with these kids. Please redeem the wasted time and consequences of any poor parenting decisions. If there are hard issues which need to be discussed before the wedding, give us the words to say and the opportunity to say them. Heal hurts and draw us closer as we draw closer to you.

Teach us all to operate from a place of forgiveness and grace and to treasure the short time we have together.

For my son(s), I pray a special measure of understanding as his sister is so distracted during this time. Keep his heart soft as he watches his sister head toward the altar. Remind him to pray for and encourage her as the responsibility of becoming a wife looms ahead. Help my son(s) with his upcoming wedding responsibilities. May there be no hurt feelings or bitterness which comes from unmet expectations or misunderstandings. Help a special friendship to grow between him and his new brother-in-law.

For my daughter(s), I pray protection over her heart as her sister moves on to a new phase in her life. Please help her to feel included and needed in the wedding planning and execution. Draw our girls closer together while they negotiate this new path and their changing relationship. Please give her and her new brother-in-law a strong foundation as friends, with healthy boundaries and unconditional love for each other.

May my children love each other and love you, Lord, with unending joy.

Help me to be aware of hidden problems which may be upsetting any of my children, and give me the time to sit and listen. I beg for the wisdom of the Holy Spirit as I continue to parent these, my most treasured assets. With a full heart, amen.

Something Borrowed

Youth fades; love droops; the leaves of friendships fall;

A mother's secret hope outlives them all.

Oliver Wendell Holmes

Day 24 – Legalese, Please

It's not a very romantic notion, but with less than a month to go, legal details related to the upcoming nuptials are about as vital an element as you'll find. Besides the all-important marriage license itself, there is likely a litany of contracts, passports, venue licenses, and one important name change. This legal paperwork can be confusing, frustrating, and even expensive. If not completed properly and on time, so much of it has the potential to derail plans and festivities. It's time to pray for God's mercy on all the legalities tied up in the wedding preparation, execution, and following days.

Lord, how funny it is that these things which seem so unimportant in an eternal sense are so pivotal to a successful wedding celebration. Thank you for caring about every little detail of our lives and for your hand of protection over our family and that of the groom as we move forward.

For those who are traveling, I pray that all the needed paperwork is in place. May there be no issues with passports or visas for either visiting guests or for the couple as they honeymoon. Provide calm wisdom and discernment as plans are made and bags are packed. May each one have the identification required for travel. May there be no delays or disappointments caused by incorrect or misplaced travel documents.

Keep the couple vigilant regarding the need to get marriage license paperwork in order. Provide clear information about the timing of the application process and give them the opportunity to get that done without causing additional stress on their schedules.

After the ceremony, give the presiding clergy the chance to get all the required signatures. Draw a clear line of responsibility for who is to file what paperwork to make sure the marriage is recorded legally in a timely fashion. Help everyone involved to stay organized and conscientious about completing the task of filing the correct documents.

If my daughter is changing her name, have mercy as she researches and navigates the necessary red tape to make that happen. Give her patience as she communicates with government agencies, financial agencies, and professional contacts. Open up her schedule and make the procedure for getting a new driver's license or ID painless for her. Please provide graciously for all the expenses related to the name change.

For any contract paperwork relating to the wedding or reception venue or services, I pray for clarity for all involved. May there be no misunderstandings regarding fulfillment of contracts, payments, or responsibilities. May we choose only honest vendors with the best intentions, and have the ability to fulfill our end of any agreements made.

Keep me organized and give me time and resources to complete any documentation that is my responsibility. Thank you again, Father, for caring about every little detail of our lives. Amen.

Something Borrowed

Then saith he unto them, Render therefore unto
Caesar the things which are Caesar's; and unto God the
things that are God's. When they had heard these words,
they marveled, and left him, and went their way.

Matthew 22:21-22 (KJV)

Day 23 – Look Out

As we sit among the ribbons and bells and anticipate the pomp and ceremony on the horizon, there sometimes comes a tendency to overlook the suffering world around us. We may simply forget to update a prayer list, check on a neighbor, or make that contribution to the homeless shelter. We may even be so distracted we miss a chance to share an encouraging word or smile with an overwrought young mom at the grocery store. May it never be! May this season of abundance and blessing in our family's life overflow with the Holy Spirit's love and generosity to all with whom we come in contact.

Let's take seriously the words from the Gospel of Matthew, chapter 5, verses 14 through 16: "You are the light of the world. A city set on a hill cannot be hidden; nor does anyone light a lamp and put it under a basket, but on the lampstand, and it gives light to all who are in the house. Let your light shine before men in such a way that they may see your good works, and glorify your Father who is in heaven."

Father, how I long to glorify you and share your love with a broken and dying world. None of that has changed just because I am busy buying gifts and making hair appointments. Forgive me for the self-absorption which threatens to suffocate right now. Help me to look beyond my own blessings and problems and take notice of others' needs which still abound in the midst of my frantic pace.

Give me opportunities to encourage my husband, daughter, and all my family to stay others-centered even as we head full speed toward the wedding day. Create enough margin in our schedules to be able to follow your leading in lending a kind word or a hand to someone in need. Send your gentle reminders when we should stop and pray. Bring to mind your holy words as you soften our hearts and quicken our minds to reach out to others:

"Be devoted to one another in brotherly love; give preference to one another in honor." Romans 12:10

"Do not look out for your own personal interests, but also for the interests of others." Philippians 2:4

"And do not neglect doing good and sharing, for with such sacrifices God is pleased." Hebrews 13:16

Thank you for helping me refocus with an eternal lens on the world's people you love so much. For those in my family who are suffering today, I pray. For those in my church with burdens to bear, I pray. For my dear friends in pain, I pray. For my neighbors who live in darkness, I pray. For leaders in my city and country, I pray. Lord, thank you for hearing my prayers today. Amen.

Something Borrowed

Kindness has converted more sinners than either zeal, eloquence, or learning.

F. W. Faber

Day 22 – Make an Appearance

Over the last months and weeks you have been focusing on your daughter's trousseau—gown shopping, accessorizing, and outfitting her for the honeymoon. However, at this point fine-tuning your appearance should be moving up on the priority list. As you make hair and nail decisions and appointments, have final dress fittings, or take an afternoon in search of the elusive comfortable-yet-stylish shoes, ask the Lord to come along and give you peace, wisdom, and success in your efforts. He cares for you, daughter—from every blemish and run in your hose, to every anxious or ugly thought—and he wants you to feel beautiful as you take your place on the front row and celebrate the day your family begins a new chapter.

Lord, as I rush around making lists and choosing makeup colors, help me never lose track of what's going on in my heart and spirit. I beg you to keep close in my mind the truth of 1 Peter 3:3-4: "Your adornment must not be merely external—braiding the hair, and wearing gold jewelry, or putting on dresses; but let it be the hidden person of the heart, with the imperishable quality of a gentle and quiet spirit, which is precious in the sight of God."

Forgive me for any prideful, selfish, self-deprecating, or other negative feelings about my appearance which have distracted me from the truth of your love and acceptance. Help me not to entertain obsessive thoughts or compare my appearance to others in any way. May no lies of the enemy about my weight, body shape, hairstyle, or other physical attributes echo in my mind to make me feel less than beautiful during this time.

Help me to honor my daughter's wishes regarding the tone of the wedding and my expected attire. Please provide all the perfect puzzle pieces of my appearance for the remaining parties, rehearsal dinner, and the wedding day itself. Line up just the right clothes, shoes, and accessories as I finish shopping. Provide reasonably priced items and the resources to purchase them without needless debt. I beg for the provision of wise style counselors, and skilled hair stylists and makeup artists if I need help in those areas.

Above all, I desire to be precious in your sight because of the gentle and quiet spirit you so willingly supply. When I look back at photos of the wedding day, may the memories reflect not only the pleasure the outward beauty afforded, but also the unmistakable glory visible due to the radiance of your magnificent spirit. Amen.

Something Borrowed

I pray Thee, O God, that I may be beautiful within.

Socrates

Day 21 – Sweet Incense

Three weeks to go! Can you believe it? Are you panicked, or just so excited you are already having trouble sleeping? Hopefully you have been including praise and thanksgiving along with the many requests you have brought to God over the past couple of months. What joy and energy it brings our hearts to simply focus on heaven's throne room and put our concerns aside for a few minutes. We are doing what we were created to do when we turn our spirits heavenward and simply pour out our devotion to and admiration for our King. You may even want to crank up some praise music as we join the Sons of Korah in their song of joy to the Lord from Psalm 47:

"O clap your hands, all peoples;

Shout to God with the voice of joy.

For the Lord Most High is to be feared,

A great King over all the earth.

He subdues peoples under us

And nations under our feet.

He chooses our inheritance for us,

The glory of Jacob whom He loves.

God has ascended with a shout,

The Lord, with the sound of a trumpet.

Sing praises to God, sing praises;

Sing praises to our King, sing praises.

For God is the King of all the earth;

Sing praises with a skillful psalm.

God reigns over the nations,

God sits on His holy throne.

The princes of the people have assembled themselves as

the people of the God of Abraham,

For the shields of the earth belong to God;

He is highly exalted."

Lord, I come to you today with praise and thanksgiving on my lips. Thank you for being present in my heart, my home, my church, and the world around me. Thank you for revealing yourself in the colors of a sunset and the sound of a dove's coo. Thank you for the beauty I see when I look out the window and when I look into the faces of my children. Thank you for defeating death and sharing the gift of your spirit which breathes new life. Thank you for your peace which "surpasses all comprehension" and guards my heart and mind (Philippians 4:7), no matter how the turmoil in the world threatens to overwhelm me. Thank you for the holy words from Psalm 150 which echo through my mind today:

"Praise the Lord!

Praise God in His sanctuary;

Praise Him in His mighty expanse.

Praise Him for His mighty deeds;

Praise Him according to His excellent greatness.

Praise Him with trumpet sound;

Praise Him with harp and lyre.

Praise Him with timbrel and dancing;

Praise Him with stringed instruments and pipe.

Praise Him with loud cymbals;

Praise Him with resounding cymbals.

Let everything that has breath praise the Lord.

Praise the Lord!"

With a heart bursting, and your name on my lips, amen.

Something Borrowed

May my prayer be counted as incense before You;

The lifting up of my hands as the evening offering.

Psalm 141:2

Day 20 – Unbelievable

As each wedding has a unique combination of elements—color scheme, musical selection, overall atmosphere—oftentimes a singular circumstance you could have never imagined inserts itself in your plans. Perhaps there has been an unexpected death or a terminal illness diagnosis. Perhaps discord in another family marriage has been revealed. Perhaps a natural disaster has destroyed your venue. Perhaps an unplanned pregnancy is threatening to alter not only the bride's waistline, but the tone of the marriage celebration.

If an unimaginable circumstance has arisen in your family, you will naturally tend to worry. The truth is, you have no control over it, but God does. Whatever is heavy on your heart today, stop the negative drain on your limited energy, bring your burden to the throne of grace, and leave it there. If you have been blessed with smooth sailing up to this point, by all means get on your knees in thanksgiving and pray for your fellow mothers of the bride who are in distress around the world today.

Lord, my heart is broken over this circumstance. Sometimes I think I could cry for days. My only consolation is that "the Lord is near to the brokenhearted, and saves those who are crushed in spirit" Psalm 34:18. Thank you for the tender loving care, comfort, and hope only you can provide. My family and I may be "afflicted in every way, but (we are) not crushed; perplexed, but not despairing; persecuted, but not forsaken; struck down, but not destroyed..." 2 Corinthians 4:8-9. We are not destroyed, thanks to the blood of Christ. I beg for your mercy to cover us as we move forward.

If this crisis is the result of someone's sin, create in me a forgiving heart and the words and opportunity to express my love and acceptance.

The strong emotions are clouding my judgment, and I rely on you to give me uncluttered thinking as we make adjustments to deal with this unforeseen situation. Give me the sensitivity to navigate this highly-charged atmosphere. I beg for an eternal perspective as any changes are made and my expectations for the event cease to be a priority.

Make me keenly aware of the impact this crisis is having on my daughter. Reveal to me if the situation is creating an enormous distraction in my mind and heart, and help me to check in with her on a regular basis and focus on her well-being, regardless of the energy I'm expending in dealing with the problem.

Provide wisdom to my daughter and her fiancé as they add this emotional burden to the already stressful transition period they are experiencing. Draw them closer to you and to each other and provide creativity and unity as they negotiate changes to their plans. Mold this into an opportunity to strengthen their relationship and that of their extended families.

I affirm your hand of providence in my family and echo Job's wise humility: "Though he slay me, yet I will trust in him..." Job 13:15 (KJV). Amen.

Something Borrowed

Have Thine own way, Lord! Have Thine own way!

Thou art the Potter, I am the clay.

Mold me and make me after Thy will,

While I am waiting, yielded and still.

Have Thine Own Way, Lord, Adelaide A. Pollard

Day 19 – Butterfly Kisses

Hopefully your daughter's father has been included in many of your prayers as you have worked through this book, but today let's focus on this special man. Is he feeling many of the same turbulent emotions roiling through your heart? Is he concerned about mounting costs associated with the pricey event? Is he unsure how to create healthy patterns of communication with your daughter as her new household forms? The answers are likely yes, yes, a thousand times, yes—this is his baby girl we are talking about! Get on your knees now, and ask God to pour out his spirit on the father of the bride.

(If you are not married to your daughter's father, or for some reason he won't be participating in the ceremony, pray for the stepfather, grandfather, or other father figure who will fill that vital role.)

Lord, from the day our precious little girl entered our lives we have not been the same. I am thankful that she has had a childhood filled with the guidance and nurturing of a father and other godly men. I pray now for this special man as we head into these next few weeks of emotional white water. Be his comfort and steady him when the waves of joy and grief wash over him. Give me a sensitive spirit and the words or actions to comfort him as well.

I beg you to provide solutions to any conflicts which would threaten the unity and peace we desire at this cherished time in our lives. Make our relationship healthy and whole so we might face these events with clarity. If he and our daughter have any unresolved emotional issues between them, provide wisdom and opportunities for godly resolutions. May father and daughter be blessed to enter the wedding week with no strife to taint their memories.

Give him the opportunity to plan ahead and consider his words for the toasts. Please provide sharp thinking and just the right things to say to honor and bless our daughter and her groom. Give him confidence to deliver the speeches and take part in the ceremony in any way the couple asks him to. May his words and actions during the festivities be glorifying to you, Lord.

Help him to create healthy boundaries with our daughter and her new husband as they strike out on their own. Give him the knowledge to know when to give advice and when to keep quiet and pray.

May his relationship with our daughter continue to be covered with your hand of blessing after the wedding and in the years ahead. May they enjoy each other's company and be a beacon of love and friendship bound together by your spirit. If and when the day comes for him to become a grandfather, bring him tremendous joy and the ability to support and encourage our daughter in her parenting.

For the blessing of a father you have provided my daughter, I am so grateful. Amen.

Something Borrowed

...There glides no day of gentle bliss

More soothing to the heart than this!

No thoughts of fondness e'er appear

More fond, than those I write of here!

No name can e'er on tablet shine,

My father! more beloved than thine!

To My Father on His Birthday, Elizabeth Barrett
Browning

Day 18 – Beloved

It's no secret that the enemy of our souls bombards your daughter with fiery arrows intended to damage and destroy her self-esteem. Everywhere she turns, she faces false images and unrealistic comparisons which erode the firm foundation of confidence you have endeavored to build in her spirit. Even if your sweet girl is feeling on top of the world while planning life with the man of her dreams, she may have thoughts of unworthiness which will threaten to steal her joy in the coming days. If your daughter has put her faith in Jesus Christ, she has a unique role in the Kingdom of God, and needs her position there affirmed. (If she has yet to take that step, pray for her in faith, for we see clearly in 1 Timothy 2:4 that God desires all to be saved.) If you are struggling with your own thoughts of self-doubt, pray for yourself along with your daughter today as you claim God's promises as his child.

Lord, as my precious girl begins to navigate her way in this world without me at her side, give her healthy beliefs about herself and her role in your kingdom. Forgive me for the times I have not modeled a sense of self-worth in line with my position as your child. Forgive me for words or attitudes of mine which have served to diminish her in any way.

Today, I ask you to silence the voice of the enemy which would tear my daughter down with lies about her appearance, intelligence, worthiness, or even her salvation. May your voice be the one she hears, regardless of her negative feelings, unhealthy thought patterns, or past experiences. May she not look to others for affirmation or approval, but know that you alone are enough. Stamp on her heart these truths:

She has been chosen by God and is holy and beloved: "This is how much God loved the world: He gave his Son, his one and only Son" (John 3:16, The Message).

She is a child of God, a treasured daughter of the King of Kings: "But as many as received Him, to them He gave the right to become children of God, even to those who believe in His name" (John 1:12).

She is wholly accepted and free from condemnation: "Therefore there is now no condemnation for those who are in Christ Jesus" (Romans 8:1).

She has the very mind of Christ: "...but we have the mind of Christ" (1 Corinthians 2:16).

She has a spirit of power, and love, and self-control: "For God hath not given us a spirit of fear, but of power, and of love, and of a sound mind" (2 Timothy 1:7, KJV).

She is a unique part of the Body of Christ: "Now you (collectively) are Christ's body, and individually (you are) members of it (each with his own special purpose and function) (1 Corinthians 12:27, AMP).

She is God's masterpiece: "For we are God's handiwork, created in Christ Jesus to do good works, which God prepared in advance for us to do" (Ephesians 2:10, NIV).

May she draw her self-worth from your love and may that confidence spill out into every aspect of her life, to your glory and honor. Amen.

Something Borrowed

And do not be conformed to this world, but be transformed by the renewing of your mind, so that you may prove what the will of God is, that which is good and acceptable and perfect.

Romans 12:2

Day 17 – Fine-Tuning Days

Now that the serious countdown to go-time has begun, you should be paying special attention to the logistical details of your responsibilities. Depending on the scope of the event, that might include anything from typing up a day-of-ceremony schedule for your family, to negotiating a who's-riding-with-whom rehearsal dinner transportation plan. Have you asked a neighbor to let your dog out on the big day (you will be gone for many, many hours)? Have you assigned a last-minute contact for the rehearsal dinner venue (you will be unavailable because of the rehearsal)? Do you have a plan for the care and feeding of any houseguests you are hosting? Whether you are a naturally organized person or not, God's wisdom regarding the fine points of the nuptial events is a must.

Lord, I come to you today with a mind crawling with information and ask you to help me sort it out. First, please help me focus on you with thanksgiving as I trust you to organize the details. Thank you for providing so abundantly the time and resources we have needed thus far to make these wedding plans come together. Thank you for the health and stamina you continue to provide our family. Thank you for the opportunity to honor my daughter and her future husband, and to honor you through the recognition of the sanctity of marriage. Thank you for all the fun we are going to have together!

I know you are a God of peace and not confusion (1 Corinthians 14:33) and ask you to fill my mind with well-ordered thoughts today. Please give me the time and energy to sort through my responsibilities and ensure tasks are covered and lines of communication are humming. Help me not to overlook any treasured family traditions or special requests my daughter has made. Help me be realistic about what I can accomplish in the next couple weeks, and to ask for help when I need it. If I already have too much assistance, give me patience and the strength to say "no thank you" in the kindest way possible.

Thank you for providing clear thinking as my emotions begin to crest and sleep is harder to come by. Thank you for helping me be prepared so fuzzy thoughts won't derail any important plans. Provide the resources and counselors to help me finish strong as the mother of the bride.

If there is anything I am neglecting to do, or any way I can help the groom or his family, please bring those things to mind. Keep me from overstepping my boundaries in any way. Mold my heart and mind, as well as my mouth, to accept and support their decisions with love.

Lord, I acknowledge that no matter how well-organized things are, there will be hiccups as we move through the wedding events. Give me the grace to respond to the stress of the unexpected with such peace and panache that my reactions will point back to you. I pray all these things for your glory, amen.

Something Borrowed

It takes as much energy to wish as it does to plan.

Eleanor Roosevelt

Day 16 – Be at Peace with All

When you anticipate the celebration to come, does the thought of interacting with one particular friend or family member create a surge of stomach acid? Is there some special soul who loves to cause turmoil, complain incessantly, or who simply doesn't seem to like you? It could be a family member or a key part of the wedding team whose anger or negativity regularly threatens to suffocate everyone around them. Dealing with this difficult person may be the biggest test you will face in allowing the Holy Spirit to control your mind and emotions (and mouth).

Remember how you began this prayer journey with the desire to be a mother of the bride who is grace-filled, peaceful, and imbued with a spirit that is pleasing to God? Now is the time to think through your interactions with that difficult person, and purpose to allow the mind of Christ to guide you at every turn. Let no plans of the enemy ruin memories of your daughter's celebration and negate any of the work the Holy Spirit has been doing in you these past weeks. Perhaps there is a special verse you could memorize and call on when that person walks into the room. Ask for Christ's mercy and intervention in this relationship today.

Lord, I think of the Apostle Paul's inspired words in Romans 12, verses 14 and 18: "Bless those who persecute you; bless and do not curse...If possible, so far as it depends on you, be at peace with all men." I confess to you today that I dread seeing this person and fear the negativity he or she will bring to our celebration. I ask your forgiveness for any part I play in keeping our relationship from being a healthy one. Please give me the wisdom to clearly see how my actions make things worse when we are together, and give me the grace to change my behavior.

Your word speaks clearly about how to respond to those who cause problems in my life, Lord. I am not only to "tolerate" them, but to love and pray for them (Matthew 5:44). I pray now for this person. I ask your spirit to intercede for me because I'm not even sure how to pray, but please bless and draw him or her closer to you.

Please keep me from the temptation to allow this person to control my emotions, and to blame any of my poor choices in word or deed on their presence at the wedding. Put a guard around my mouth as I speak about and with this person. May I speak only your words. Father, prevent me from being sucked down with my own complaints and gossip. Keep renewing my mind that I may prove your good and perfect will (Romans 12:2). As this is likely not the time or place for any type of confrontation, please give me self-control when I fear I won't be able to harness my tongue. I desire to be merciful, as you are merciful. I desire to please you, Father, and live as your beloved daughter.

No matter what may happen as a result of our interactions in the coming weeks and days, keep the truth of 1 Thessalonians 5:15 resonating in my mind: "Be patient with each person, attentive to individual needs. And be careful that when you get on each other's nerves you don't snap at each other. Look for the best in each other, and always do your best to bring it out" (The Message). Amen.

Something Borrowed

If we could read the secret history of our enemies, we should find in each man's life sorrow and suffering enough to disarm all hostility.

Henry Wadsworth Longfellow

Day 15 – Blessing Your Daughter

The Bible is steeped in the tradition and symbolism of the act of bestowing blessings. Beyond simple intercession, blessing children is a powerful tool of affirmation and a declaration of a parent's vision. It gives a voice to the ability of God's promises to positively impact the one being blessed.

If you have never taken the time to formally pray words of affirmation and encouragement over your daughter, or even if you have, go to the Lord today and ask him to open the floodgates of heaven on this young woman's behalf. Today's prayer may be prayed individually, or you may want to intercede with your husband on behalf of your daughter. You may even wish to write your own blessing which more specifically addresses her individual personality and situation. In addition, you can take it one step further and write a blessing for your daughter and future son-in-law as a way of supporting their union. Tuck a copy of this blessing in your purse so if you have the opportunity to steal a few private moments with the bride on her wedding day, you may create a treasured memory together.

Father God, I come to you today remembering how you spoke precious words of blessing even over your one and only son (Mark 1:11). Following your holy example, I look to you now as a mother standing between heaven and earth on behalf of her child. This woman whom I love and treasure, I know you love and treasure infinitely more. May she know the high value you place on her life and soul—such a high price that it was paid for by Christ's blood. Teach her to love you more each day of her life as she grows "in the grace and knowledge of our Lord and Savior Jesus Christ" (2 Peter

3:18). Even as I see the fruits of your spirit manifested in her heart, may those fruits continue to multiply and flourish daily in her words and actions.

Bless my daughter with a long life, full of the bounty of the earth and the goodness of heaven. May your angels guard and guide her at every turn, as she lies down or walks on the road. May she never lose the correct perspective of eternity, but continually strive to store up treasures where no moth or rust can destroy, or thieves break in and steal (Matthew 6:19). I pray that my daughter will look to you always as her source of every good and perfect gift, heeding the call of God through the psalmist: "Open your mouth wide and I will fill it" Psalm 81:10b.

I pray that as my daughter moves through life she will emulate our savior in humility and love for others (Matthew 5:16). May a sound mind and wisdom from above direct her decisions and ever steady her on the straight path. May her cup overrun with joy in all circumstances. May her children's children rise up to bless her in her old age.

I say to my daughter today, "The Lord bless you, and keep you; The Lord make His face shine on you, And be gracious to you; The Lord lift up His countenance on you, And give you peace" Numbers 6:24-26. Amen.

Something Borrowed

I remember my mother's prayers and they have always followed me. They have clung to me all my life.

Abraham Lincoln

Day 14 – Details, Details

Two weeks to go! By now your to-do list is as long as your arm, and you may be starting to panic because it's clear some things may not get done. Tasks which once seemed small may be threatening to crush your peace as the hours tick by. Should you use seat assignments and place cards at the reception? Have you made the corsage and boutonniere list (don't forget anyone!)? If you are typing up the program, have you double-checked the spelling of the attendants' names? Should you call Aunt Jane who hasn't RSVP'd and make sure she received her invitation? We surely need the Lord's help in order to take care of so many tiny, yet potentially key, details. Let's ask for it!

Wow, Lord, this is harder than I imagined. I am just the mom, after all. How did this get to be so much work? I pray for the groom's mother, who is likely feeling similar pressure at this moment. Give her peace and great energy today as she works through her list of tasks. Bring to my mind any way I can help alleviate her stress and encourage her. Help me to follow through on any promptings of your spirit to do so.

I pray also for my daughter and her groom-to-be who are not only dealing with wedding preparations, but also moving, honeymoon plans, and maybe even the complication of new jobs or schools. Keep me one step ahead of my tasks so I am available to help them if the situation arises.

Please give me clear thinking and wise prioritization of the things I must accomplish in the next two weeks. Keep my eyes on you with a firm eternal perspective. Keep me from being ruled by emotions which may have a negative impact on anyone around me. Please create a supportive atmosphere for me at work during these next few days, and give me a realistic view of any extra time off I will need to arrange.

As I consider travel arrangements, weather issues, gifts, clothes and shoes, venue confirmations, deposit money, hairdos, flowers, set-up and clean-up help, and the myriad other categories ticking through my mind, make me diligent, but not obsessive. Give me enough of a time margin to deal with any unexpected tasks that will surely come along.

As this time of little sleep and the possibility of roadblocks goes by, keep my mind focused on you. Help me not to borrow trouble from tomorrow, "...for tomorrow will care for itself" (Matthew 6:34). Make your word and your peace the loudest sounds in my mind. Amen.

Something Borrowed

For I am confident of this very thing, that He who began a good work in you will perfect it until the day of Christ Jesus.

Philippians 1:6

Day 13 – Celebrate Good Times

As you continue to consider how your family dynamic will transform over the coming months, it's a good time to work through expectations when it comes to holidays. Have you *always* taken your daughter out for breakfast on her birthday? Or have you *always* opened gifts and gone to church as a family on Christmas Eve? Do all your children *always* gather together on Labor Day? These schedules may not necessarily fit in with the blossoming traditions your daughter and her new husband will begin with their little family unit. They may not work out when taking her in-laws' schedules and traditions into consideration. Now is the time to examine your heart and to let go of any expectations and the potential for hurt feelings during these festive days of joy.

Heavenly Father, thank you that you are God of celebration. We praise you that you want us to rest and play and eat good food to commemorate the wonderful things you have done for us. Thank you for the abundance of time and resources you provide so we may have these singular moments together. Thank you for the precious memories of holidays with my little girl you have allowed me to store up in my heart. Thank you for the new family she will be joining and the wonderful times they have in store together.

I ask you to help me examine my heart when it comes to holiday traditions. Shine a light on any areas of potential selfishness or childishness that lurk in the corners of my emotions. Remind me that holiday seasons are not a competition, but a celebration of generosity, especially with my time. Give me a clear view of the pressures my newly-married children are facing from every angle when it comes to pleasing all their relatives. I beg for great discernment in how I use my words and express my needs and desires during holidays.

Give my daughter and her new husband courage to say no (even to me). Provide the resources, focus, and energy they need to create their own special memories together. Help them build their celebrations around you, Lord, and the blessings you have provided. Give my daughter wisdom to support her groom and consider his needs above her own. Help my new son-in-law feel included and irreplaceable as we gather for holiday celebrations.

As we continue to add to our family through the birth of grandchildren or the weddings of our other children, give me the skills to plan carefully so no schedule mishaps occur that might derail a planned event. Give me grace to be flexible as we begin to build new traditions in our expanding family unit. Provide abundant creativity so we can continue to make holiday memories to last a lifetime.

Above all, Lord, help me to remember that birthdays, civic holidays, and spiritual celebrations are all gifts from you. Keep my family and me focused on your face as we experience the rejuvenation and joy these special times provide. Amen.

Something Borrowed

A thing of beauty is a joy forever:

Its loveliness increases; it will never

Pass into nothingness; but still will keep

A bower quiet for us, and a sleep

Full of sweet dreams, and health, and quiet breathing.

John Keats

Day 12 – Flood of Tears

It comes like a flood—often unbidden, unexpected, unwanted. Even if you are not an "emotional" person, it will likely show up at least once in the next days. Gut-wrenching, heartbreaking, tissue-soaking grief may bubble to the surface when you least expect it. And like a deluge, the churning, cleansing floodwaters of grief strip away the old and reveal the new. In this instance, the tears are a relief valve put in place by Creator God to ensure you won't attempt to skate through these powerful circumstances without acknowledging your feelings. So besides having waterproof makeup at the ready and knowing where the tissue box is in each room, let's ask the Holy Spirit to comfort and guide through the tumultuous moments to come.

Oh Lord, how my emotions are threatening to rise up out of nowhere and sabotage me at the least opportune moment! I know you understand, and I trust you to guide me through this process.

Thank you so much, God, for the privilege of having these sweet mothering memories. Thank you for my daughter and each minute, hour, day, and year we have logged together on this earth. Thank you for the postcard-perfect times of peace and joy. Thank you for the terrible, horrible, very bad days and bringing us through them.

Help me to sort through this unfathomably deep sadness when I consider the fact that my family is changing and will never, ever, be the same. Fill me with your spirit as I watch my little girl turn her face away from her father and me to begin a new life apart from us. Comfort me, Lord! Look down in mercy on me! Hold me close as I cry. Whisper in my ear the truth that each of my tears is so precious to you that you hold them in a bottle (Psalm 56:8). Bring to mind your steadfast words of hope as I add to that bottle.

Give me the courage to be vulnerable with my husband and daughter as I sort through these feelings. Please provide them with the wisdom to comfort without feeling like they need to provide a solution to my sadness. If it would be appropriate for me to voice my sorrow to my daughter without casting a shadow over her week, please supply the time, place, and the words to say. Help her to know how much I love her and how happy I am for her, even when I sometimes wish time would stand still.

Lord, you know my heart's desire is for my family to be centered on you in healthy relationships. Give me mature, balanced thoughts in the coming hours and days as I think about and feel these emotions which threaten to smother me. Help me not to ignore these feelings, but to move through them and into the bright future you have for me and my relationship with my daughter. I am so looking forward to the laughter and joyful new memories to come. In the strong and merciful name of Jesus I pray, amen.

Something Borrowed

To weep, is to make less the depth of grief.

William Shakespeare

Day 11 – One in the Spirit

You will likely be raising a glass to the health of the bride and groom at the coming dinners and receptions, but have you considered toasting their spiritual health? Nothing is more precious than a married couple sharing their spiritual journey together with transparency and vulnerability. And nothing is a bigger target for the enemy than a healthy marriage and the spiritual fruit it can produce. Even if you don't feel you have modeled this well, it's never too late to ask God to change your attitudes and actions and redeem the mistakes you have made. Pray today that your daughter and her groom will move together toward wholeness and maturity in Jesus Christ, securing their bond in love, and serving as a beacon of reconciliation to a dying world.

Father, thank you for the privilege of praying for my daughter and her husband-to-be as they begin this new life together. Thank you for trusting me to be the mother of this woman, and for generously providing discernment to raise her under the guidance of your spirit and holy word. Forgive me for the many times I have fallen short in displaying the fruit of your spirit. Forgive me for the unintentional mistakes and the overt disobedience this young woman has observed in my life. Give me the courage to apologize, and the strength to change my behavior where necessary. I know the impact of my actions far outweighs that of my words, and I beg for your conviction and guidance in any areas which need to be corrected.

I pray that my daughter and new son-in-law would begin their marriage with hearts full of forgiveness toward one another. Train them to keep short accounts and to learn healthy ways of dealing with conflicts and misunderstandings. May no anger or shame come between them and discourage their transparency as they pray together. May my daughter always respect her husband, so that even if he is "disobedient to the word," he may be "won without a word" by her behavior (1 Peter 3:1). Create a powerful spiritual force in their union as they come to the throne of heaven together.

Please give this sweet couple a hunger and thirst for Scripture, striving to meditate, study, and apply your principles for life and freedom each day of their marriage. Bring them excellent teachers and opportunities for learning, and remind them to rely on your spirit of revelation as they open your perfect word. May it be a source of joy and encouragement for them as they move through the ups and downs of life, and give them an immovable hope for a heavenly future.

May they always have a healthy church family to call their own, filled with godly friends, wise teachers and counselors, and opportunities to serve others. No matter the circumstances, keep alive in their hearts the truth of Hebrews 10:24-25: "and let us consider how to stimulate one another to love and good deeds, not forsaking our own assembling together, as is the habit of some, but encouraging one another; and all the more as you see the day drawing near."

A toast from my heart to yours, Jesus, on behalf of my children. Keep them close. Amen.

Something Borrowed

I stand amazed in the presence

Of Jesus the Nazarene,

And wonder how He could love me,

A sinner condemned, unclean.

How marvelous! how wonderful!

And my song shall ever be:

How marvelous! how wonderful!

Is my Savior's love for me!

I Stand Amazed, Charles H. Gabriel

Day 10 – No Boys Allowed

The day of the bachelorette party is probably drawing near at this point. Whether your daughter's friends are planning a big evening out, or even a weekend getaway, what a special time for them to commemorate her final days of singleness. It is a beautiful opportunity for these friends to reminisce and to honor a special young bride, while celebrating the institution of marriage. However, if some of your daughter's friends tend toward the wild side, this event has the potential to create unfavorable memories and problems nobody wants to deal with. Let's pray God's hand of protection on the ladies as they cut loose and have fun—no boys allowed!

Father, thank you for these extraordinary women who love my daughter and consider her a friend. Thank you that they have chosen to celebrate her by investing so much of their time, energy, and money into being involved in her wedding. As they plan and execute the bachelorette party, give them wisdom and the opportunity to create a festive atmosphere and unique memories they can carry with them for the rest of their lives. Give them ingenuity to plan things to do that would be enjoyable for everyone. Give them the financial resources to pull it off, and don't allow the expenses to become a burden to any of them. Help them to communicate well so everyone knows in advance where the party will be held and when to arrive.

Provide a leader who will take responsibility for scheduling and assigning tasks for the festivities so nothing is left to the last minute. Please don't allow any bullying or hard feelings as the planning takes place. As this is clearly not my responsibility, protect me from the urge to make sure things are being done the way I would like to see them done. Show me if I can be helpful, but don't let me embarrass myself or my daughter by being intrusive.

Guide the bride as she chooses special mementos for her bridesmaids. Give her sentimental and unique ideas which fit her budget. Please allow her a tender moment with each young woman as she distributes the gifts.

Keep the young women from the temptation or opportunity for any activity that would not be honoring to you. Guard and protect them as they come and go. Help my daughter to feel honored and loved and to properly express her appreciation for the hard work and expense her friends will be expending. Give me the initiative to check in with her the next day and allow her to reminisce about the fun times with her girlfriends.

I ask you to provide in a similar fashion for the groom and his friends while they celebrate. As yet another expenditure is added to their plates, supply all their needs. Provide creativity and unity among all the friends who are planning and attending. Help my future son-in-law to feel extremely loved.

Keep my daughter, her fiancé, and all their friends safe and joyful as they remember and celebrate their singleness one last time. Create opportunities for them to stay connected with healthy friendships even after the wedding, encouraging and loving each other through all of life's transformations. Amen.

Something Borrowed

Hand

Grasps hand, eye lights eye in good friendship,

And great hearts expand,

And grow one in the sense of this world's life.

Robert Browning

Day 9 – Shaping a Legacy

Your mom or even your grandmother may still be living, but have you ever considered how you will be remembered in your maternal roles after your death? Legacies are not created in a day, a year, or even a decade, but are the culmination of a lifetime of choices. As a Christian mother, does the heritage you are crafting reflect your love for Christ and his bride, the church (Ephesians 5:22-23)? Are you being purposeful to spend your time wisely in prayer, study, service, and relationship-building as you are led by the Holy Spirit? Will those who remember your life have any doubt about its mission? As your family continues to grow, ask God to create a vision of the eternal footprint you will someday leave behind, and give you the desire to follow his perfect will for your life.

Whew. Lord, it is a little hard to consider such a weighty matter at a time when I can barely put two sentences together. Thank you for the opportunity I have today to view things from a different perspective through the lens of my heightened emotions. Please use this time when life is not "normal" to show me things I might not realize when the daily grind has numbed my senses.

As the picture of our family expands to include more beautiful souls, I beg for a revelation of the future you have for us. Help me to see the many ways my choices can build the foundation of a godly heritage for those I love now, and for those I will love in the future. It is my desire to be a mother, grandmother, and great-grandmother who points my family to the saving grace of Jesus, and who lives with the delight of the abundant life our savior promised (John 10:10).

Father, I have made so many mistakes as a wife and mother. Please forgive me for those impatient, rebellious, selfish, foolish choices and give me the wisdom to not repeat the same errors. May no lies from the enemy deceive me or discourage me from hearing your voice of encouragement in the areas which seem impossible to change. Lord, your word says when I am in you, there is no place for condemnation, and I claim that promise today (Romans 8:1). I want to be remembered as a Christlike woman, strong in faith, devoted to love, resilient in battle, bold in reconciliation, and joyful in all things. May your gentle and quiet spirit define me as I move through the second half of life.

I ask also that you help my daughter and her groom to envision their place in our family's legacy. May they feel welcome and loved by me and everyone around our table. May they be encouraged knowing that they are being carried to heaven's throne in my prayers, and that they can count on me to love and support them through Christ's power. May their praises echo the psalmist in chapter 16, verse 6: "The lines have fallen to me in pleasant places; Indeed my heritage is beautiful to me." In Christ's eternal name I pray, amen.

Something Borrowed

But as for me, the nearness of God is my good;

I have made the Lord God my refuge,

That I may tell of all Your works.

Psalm 73:28

Day 8 – In Bright or Stormy Weather

Have you checked the forecast? If the wedding is outdoors, you likely haven't stopped glancing at the weather news since the date was announced. But whether you are dreading an ice storm, watching the skies for thunder and hail, or praying the church's air conditioning is operational, there is no denying the major role the weather will play in your upcoming week. Concerns run the gamut of seriousness. Maybe hazardous roads will threaten to keep guests away or even put them in danger. Maybe your daughter is worrying about high humidity threatening her hairdo (a huge menace in any bride's mind). Let's bring every concern to God, who not only cares about our frizzy hair, but actually knows how many of them rest on each of our heads (Luke 12:7).

Father, first of all, I acknowledge that you control the wind and the rain, the thunder and lightning. I praise you that the storehouses of snow and hail belong to you (Job 38:22). I praise you that the heat and cold obey your word, and you promise to maintain the balance of nature "while the earth remains" (Genesis 8:22).

I pray for the physical protection of all participants and guests. I ask there be no car accidents, flight delays, delivery issues, or health problems caused by the weather. May the facilities all be heated or cooled properly and the parking lots and sidewalks be clear of obstacles.

For any outdoor activities planned during the week and the special day ahead, I pray for your mercy in holding back precipitation or temperature extremes. Give us resources for alternate venues in case of unfavorable conditions. Give us the wisdom to know when and if to abandon outdoor plans. If I am not one of the decision-makers, give me the strength to keep my opinions to myself. Provide clear communication to all attendees regarding venue changes. Provide instructions for proper attire so no one is uncomfortable due to being over or underdressed.

No matter what weather may threaten, I beg you not to allow fear to ruin this delightful time for my family and friends. May we turn to you with any concerns and rely on you for good judgment as the week unfolds. Give us peace as we deal with the weather.

Please send us a great sense of humor as these things we can't control may cause unanticipated hiccups. Help us to focus on the few essential and eternal factors surrounding this day, and not let bad weather rob us of joy. Amen.

Something Borrowed

There is something good in all weathers. If it doesn't happen to be good for my work today, it's good for some other man's today and will come 'round for me tomorrow.

Charles Dickens

Day 7 – Turning the Page

Although your family truly changed the day your daughter placed the engagement ring on her finger, it may have been easy up until now to ignore the permanent shift that has taken place. As you look at the calendar today, it is clear that this is the final (insert today's day of the week) that your family will look like it has for so long. This time next week you will have a new son, and you will have officially handed over the keys to your daughter's heart. If it hasn't already, her focus will forever be changed as she heads into her future. In many ways, your point of view will move to the outside looking in, watching as she creates a new home. This is the goal of any healthy mother-daughter relationship, and likely the very thing you have prayed for since she was born. It's exciting, but sometimes it still hurts. Today, let's acknowledge the exhilaration and the pain found here at the end of this chapter in your family's story.

Lord God, I am so grateful that you heard my prayers long ago for my daughter to find a good husband. Thank you for bringing this special man into her life and for the future you have for them. Thank you for the love and joy we have experienced during their engagement, and the memories made. Thank you for the woman my daughter has become and your protection over her all these years. Thank you that I have lived to see this day.

As we look at photos and reminisce, I am struck by your faithfulness to us. It seems like just yesterday my husband and I were making plans and dreaming dreams of our own together, picking out baby names and buying tiny shoes. How that petite pink bundle changed our world! I remember some of those days seeming to last forever as one diaper change rolled into the next, and stray Barbie shoes threatened to cripple my bare feet. I remember those moments around the table in the evening, talking about schoolwork and big plans for the future. Then there were the teen years with her laser focus on friendships and the trappings of becoming a young woman. As nights around the dinner table got to be fewer and fewer, I knew this time would come. You knew this time would come too, Lord, and come it has—like a speeding locomotive.

Even though things may not have turned out exactly as we had pictured them so long ago, Lord, you have been faithful through every quiet moment and every trial. Now that we are experiencing another momentous change, adding another precious face at the table and another child to pray for, I ask that you guard my heart. Help me to balance celebration and sadness this week and to remember your goodness as the echoes of laughter and little feet fill my mind. Bring the beloved memories on, and give me strength to cry and laugh as I acknowledge those times are gone. Give me the sweet hope of new memories to be made, new margins of time and space in my life, and the possibility of filling my house with the laughter of grandchildren in your perfect time. Amen.

Something Borrowed

Ah! memories of sweet summer eves,

Of moonlit wave and willowy way,

Of stars and flowers, and dewy leaves,

And smiles and tones more dear than they!

John Greenleaf Whittier

Day 6 – Esteem Them Very Highly

Although the concept of a wedding officiant is not an element in every culture, no doubt your Western wedding will require an ordained celebrant, or an officiant with non-spiritual affiliation to oversee the ceremony. No matter your circumstance, the person directing the ceremony and the exchange of vows will be front and center. So whether it's a special relative, the pastor who baptized your daughter, or simply someone the couple hired from an online search, this man or woman needs your prayers. You may even want to send an encouraging note, telling this individual you are praying specifically for him or her today.

Lord, as we have passed the one-week mark before the wedding day, I thank you for providing so abundantly for every need and request. Thank you for caring about each detail and for speaking to every ragged thought tumbling around in my mind. Thank you for every minute I have with my daughter during these coming days, and the sweet light that sparkles in her eye when she talks about her betrothed.

Today I pray for the person who will officiate this wedding. Thank you for providing just the right individual, opening up his/her schedule, and for the key part he/she will have in the celebration. Thank you for the desire you have placed within this person to preside over the ceremony, and to become a special part of our family's history.

I pray for the officiant's physical health and that you would keep him/her strong over the coming days. As he/she prepares the order of service and the message to be delivered, provide great wisdom and insight. Allow ample opportunities and motivation for preparation and keep him/her organized as he/she prioritizes time commitments this week. Bring him/her to the altar confident and filled with your spirit.

Provide the ability and desire to craft a message that pleases you, Father. Even if this person is not a believer in Christ, I pray the words he/she utters during the service would accurately reflect your view of marriage and honor your son, Jesus.

For every physical aspect of message delivery, I pray you will guide and protect him/her. May there be no technical difficulties with audio visual equipment, electronic devices, or even old-fashioned paper. May he/she remember everything needed for the service. Keep him/her organized and on schedule, and able to find the venue without any difficulties.

May the officiant feel welcome and an honored part of the activities both on the wedding day and the days leading up to it. If there is anything I can do or say to encourage him/her or bring him/her closer to you, Lord, give me the opportunity, boldness, and the words to speak. May your love be reflected in me as we interact to create a ceremony which holds your name in highest esteem. Amen.

Something Borrowed

But we request of you, brethren, that you appreciate those who diligently labor among you, and have charge over you in the Lord and give you instruction, and that you esteem them very highly in love because of their work. Live in peace with one another.

1 Thessalonians 5:12-13

Day 5 – A Rushing Wind

Are you having trouble breathing? Between the excitement, anxiety, grief, and other turbulent emotions, are you struggling to catch your breath? God not only wants you to take deep breaths, he wants to fill you up with his cleansing spirit. He wants you to be an irrefutable walking, talking testimony of his peace and provision. As the final hours before the wedding ceremony tick by, choose to focus on the eternal. Ask God to bless you and your family with the manifestation of his spirit. Entreat him to come and permeate these next few days and the ceremony itself with the unmistakable presence of his glory.

Jehovah God, thank you for your promise to pour out your spirit on the descendants of Jacob (Isaiah 44:3). I claim that promise today as my family and I have been grafted into his line through the sacrifice of Christ (Romans 11:17-21). I am desperate for your spirit! Help me to clearly recognize and reject anything within me that keeps it from being poured out in my life. Holy Spirit, may your love, joy, peace, patience, kindness, goodness, faithfulness, gentleness, and self-control guide my thoughts, words, and actions (Galatians 5:22-23).

I pray for my precious daughter today and ask you to fill her. Have mercy on her jumbled thoughts and emotions; comfort and guide her as only you can. Drench her heart with your love as she walks through this remarkable time in her life. May your spirit's voice help her to balance joy and exuberance with wisdom. Comfort her through disappointments, and create a clear vision of the wonderful future you have in store for her and her beloved.

No matter where the exchanging of vows takes place, I beg you to come and fill that spot. Whether it be a church or a windswept beach, may your love and joy be palpable as we gather and as the ceremony progresses. Create an atmosphere of unity and peace. According to your will, I ask that your message of salvation be expressed openly and freely and revered by everyone present. Move in the hearts and minds of all in attendance. May we look back on this time and say without a doubt, "The Lord was in this place." Amen.

Something Borrowed

Yes, Thou art ever present, Power supreme!

Not circumscribed by time, nor fixed to space,

Confined to altars, nor to temples bound.

In wealth, in want, in freedom, or in chains,

In dungeons or on thrones, the faithful find Thee.

Hannah More

Day 4 – An Apple a Day

As you are closing in on the final days before the ceremony, it is time to ask for God's mercy in terms of health. Although the only people who really must be present are the bride, groom, witnesses, and officiant, what heartbreak for any who wish attend but can't, due to illness. Of course, you can do your part to stay healthy by looking for ways to bolster your immune system—remember to take your vitamins and drink lots of water, use special care in hand washing, and get some rest. But most importantly, today and every day between now and the ceremony, ask the Lord to protect you and your loved ones from any accidents or sickness.

Heavenly Father, no matter what season or what germs are being passed around in our community, I ask for your mercy as we enter public places and gather together. Give those who are ill the wisdom to stay home and not spread germs. In Jesus' name, may no germs take hold of my family or me. May the bride and groom be in perfect health for their special day. Please provide and help us to choose adequate rest and nutrition as we head into these stressful, full-to-the-brim hours ahead.

Guard my family, the groom's family, the officiant, bridal party, musicians, caterers, photographers, florists, and any who are slated to have a special part in the ceremony or reception. May there be no illness shared on the day of the wedding.

For the elderly who will be joining us, I ask that you keep them from falls or exposure to any harmful germs. For any with chronic illnesses who will be participating in our special day, I ask that you alleviate their pain or discomfort so they may enjoy the festivities to the fullest. For the littlest participants, I pray that you will keep them from picking up germs from their peers at school or daycare prior to the wedding.

Make us particularly aware of any participants or attendees with physical disabilities or special needs, such as those with hearing impairments or mobility issues. Provide insight and resources to help them enjoy their time with us.

I beg your protection from accidents as well. Send your angels to guard those traveling by car, train, or plane. May all who wish to attend the wedding find themselves in good physical condition and able to do so. If any health problems do arise, give us creative solutions and peace to deal with the situation.

Keep my daughter and her beloved in perfect health as they head out on their honeymoon and begin their life together. Provide a time of rejuvenating rest for them and for all of us during the days following the ceremony. Thank you for the gift of health. Amen.

Something Borrowed

Therefore, confess your sins to one another, and pray for one another so that you may be healed. The effective prayer of a righteous man can accomplish much.

James 5:16

Day 3 – The Practice Run

Sometime in the next day or so you will likely be taking part in the rehearsal and rehearsal dinner or other special meal. Although details of the ceremony rehearsal itself may fall squarely in your lap, responsibility for the meal following is traditionally the privilege of the groom's family. This is an opportunity for you to take a long breath and let someone else play the part of hostess. Remember to pray for the groom's mother as she may have to make last-minute adjustments to the guest list, menu, or even her wardrobe. Pray that this more intimate time with family and friends before the wedding will result in many happy memories for all involved.

Lord, as the spotlight falls on the groom's family, I am thankful for the brief respite. Be with the mother of the groom as she likely bears a heavy weight of responsibility on her shoulders today. Thank you for bringing us to this moment in the wedding process, for providing everything we have needed, and for giving us this once-in-a-lifetime opportunity to celebrate my daughter and her fiancé. Thank you for this chance to get to know our daughter's new in-laws, and to watch with tenderness as she becomes part of another family unit.

Please take charge of every detail of the rehearsal. Where I have not planned well, come behind and provide what is needed. Where I have over-planned or worried, lift my hands from the situation and keep my perspective in line with yours. Bring to mind anything that needs to be double-checked and give me organizational skills and diligence to complete those tasks. Reveal solutions to any problems which present themselves.

As the rehearsal unfolds, please allow things to go smoothly. May participants be on time and focused on their tasks; may there be a natural leader who can keep things moving along; may the officiant, musicians, and photographers use this time to prepare well for the ceremony; and may the bride and groom feel peaceful and cherished as we gather together.

Heavenly Father, provide health, safe travel, and pleasant accommodations for all the dinner guests. Make the directions to the event space clear and parking adequate. Help everyone to feel comfortable in the venue, to have lively table companions, and to enjoy the menu. Provide excellent food and servers as we celebrate. Give anyone who will toast the couple the exact right words to say and the courage to say them. If there are technical aspects of the dinner, such as special music or a slideshow, allow them to proceed flawlessly.

If there have been any misunderstandings or hurt feelings about the guest list for the event, please provide clear communication and a quick resolution. Let no bitterness be given a chance to take root in the midst of such a joyful time.

Lord, I am so exhausted! Thank you for carrying me when I can't make it another step. Give me the focus to thoroughly enjoy this day as my daughter begins the extraordinary adventure of marriage. With a grateful heart, amen.

Something Borrowed

Our praying needs to be pressed and pursued with an
energy that never tires, a persistency which will not be
denied, and courage that never fails.

E.M. Bounds

Day 2 – Pray Without Ceasing

Even if the rehearsal dinner is not on the eve of the wedding, today will be a blur. Are the tuxes picked up? Who is fetching Grandma from the airport? What options are there if the ring bearer refuses to walk down the long, scary aisle? Have you offered enough help to the sweet bride, or are you getting in the way? You may be juggling manicures and grandchildren, running errands for others, dealing with car problems or illness. Add to that the roiling emotions you must squash in order to get everything done, and you have a day that needs to be filled from start to finish with prayer. Begin with this short prayer and keep the lines of communication open with the Lord as the day progresses.

Heavenly Father, I can't do this without your guidance and strength. Fill me with your Holy Spirit today as I move through each challenge. Shine through me with your love, joy, peace, patience, kindness, goodness, faithfulness, gentleness, and self-control (Galatians 5:22-23). Help me to communicate clearly with my daughter the depth of my love for her and my excitement as she begins married life. Give me a time and place to process any emotions which bubble to the surface.

I pray that my husband and I will put aside any differences and be able to take part in this sacred event in oneness, as an example to our daughter and her new husband. Dole out an extra measure of forgiveness and grace as we move through the next couple of exhausting and stressful days. Help us to renew the unity of our hearts through the joy we see in each other and the thankfulness of your blessings on our family. Fill our other children with your spirit and give them peace as they participate in these activities.

I pray for the health and safety of every person participating in and attending the wedding and reception. Send your angels to guard and protect us as we gather together.

Thank you for every blessing you have provided up to this point. We beg for your hand of fortune to continue with us over the next twenty-four hours. Make love our watchword. Amen.

Something Borrowed

Up, up fair bride! And call thy stars from out their
several boxes; take thy rubies, pearls, and diamonds forth,
and make thyself a constellation of them all.

John Donne

Day 1 – The Day the Lord Hath Made

This will be one of the busiest days of your life. You most likely did not sleep much last night, and a thousand last-minute details may be threatening to suffocate you. But the worst thing you can do at this point is neglect prayer.

Truth is, by now the event is in motion and all you really must do is show up and direct the activity. What's done is done and the rest won't matter. So whether you do it before or after you powder your nose, get on your knees and ask God to fill you with his spirit in special measure as your family moves on to a new phase through the sacred activities of this day. You can catch up on sleep tomorrow.

Lord, hear my prayers today. My mind and emotions are on such high alert I find it hard to focus, but you promise your spirit will intercede for me anyway (Romans 8:26). Praise you for being such a loving, kind, generous God. Thank you for bringing us to this day, for the blessings of health and provision that I tend to take for granted. Thank you for the mystery of marriage and the future my daughter enters in a few hours. Thank you for the blessing of a daughter, the precious memories we share, and the love which permeates our home. Thank you for bringing her new husband into our lives, and for the expansion of our hearts as our family grows.

I cry out to you on behalf of my baby girl today, Lord! Fill her with your spirit of joy and peace as she prepares to take the most sacred of vows. May her expectations of this day be met and exceeded, and may she honor you as she begins this new phase of her life. Guard and protect her and help her to love you more each day.

Empty me of any worry, fear, anger, self-absorption, or impatience that would threaten to create negative recollections of these precious hours. Fill me with your spirit of love, joy, peace, patience, kindness, goodness, faithfulness, gentleness, and self-control (Galatians 5:22). If expectations are not met, give us your heavenly perspective. If obstacles present themselves, give us solutions. If disagreements arise, give us grace. If sickness looms, give us a reprieve of health. If grouchy people threaten to rob us of joy, close our ears.

Saturate the ceremony and reception with your spirit of truth. Give the officiant inspired words as he blesses our children. Touch any hearts that have grown cold toward you and reveal the mystery of your love for us. Give us a glimpse of the joy of the heavenly wedding banquet promised to those who put their trust in Christ's sacrifice for mankind. Be honored today and as our family moves on to the next phase of this glorious adventure. Amen and amen.

Something Borrowed

The past, the present and the future are really one: they are today.

Harriet Beecher Stowe

Epilogue – Keep Praying

It's over! A few guests may linger, dry cleaning may still be piled in a corner, boxes and bags of decorations may be overflowing your car, but for the most part, it is finished. Well done, Mama, well done. Take time over the next few days as you're catching up on sleep and writing thank-you notes to reflect on all the answers to prayer God provided over the past months. You may even want to write the Lord a message of thanksgiving to stick in your Bible as a reminder of his goodness as your family continues its transformation.

If there were unpleasant moments during the celebratory events, ask God to examine your heart and yank out any root of bitterness that may be threatening to taint your recollections of the day. Forgive as you have been forgiven. If you were guilty of a poorly-timed word or action, apologize promptly so you won't be the source of anyone else's unpleasant memory.

And it's certainly not over for the newlyweds. Since you are likely a veteran of marriage you know that things are only just beginning for your daughter and her husband. The sweet couple needs your prayers now more than ever. As they return from the honeymoon and begin the so-called "hardest year" of marriage, your job as an intercessor is vital. Difficult as it is to think about, every couple who seeks to glorify God in their marriage has an enemy. They need praying parents to help fortify their home. Even if the newlyweds have not made godly living a priority, they need your prayers to help guide them back to the right path. Make it a habit to pray for them every day.

Father in heaven, now that the wedding is over, thank you for your hand of blessing as my daughter and her husband took their vows and began their life as one. Fill their home with your presence and your grace every day. Remind them to be gentle with one another at all times because you are near (Philippians 4:5).

Keep them safe from harm as they work and play. Protect them from accidents or illness. May any unhealthy or ungodly options or activities be exposed before they cause damage. Provide abundantly for their every need through your grace. Give them good work to do and help them to do it well. Give them wisdom for every educational and career option and help them to be in agreement over the myriad choices they face. As they combine their financial resources, give them reasonable expectations and clear communication.

When they disagree or argue, give them compassion for one another and prompt them to choose their words wisely. Never let them forget who the enemy is and to take seriously the vital need to reconcile after each quarrel. Let no wall of bitterness or hardness of heart grow up between them.

May the physical aspects of their union be blessed. Give them excellent communication and keep the marriage bed pure all the days of their lives. Take away any threat to their marriage in the forms of other people, media influences, bad habits, selfishness, or addictions. Provide unity in their family planning decisions. Bless them with children in your timing.

Surround them with a group of godly friends and advisers who will encourage them to seek your face, study your word, and gather together with spiritual brothers and sisters on a regular basis. Above all, keep their faces turned to you as they meet every challenge through your grace during this first year of their marriage. Teach them to love you more each day.

Thank you for answering my prayers according to your sovereign will. Amen.

Something Borrowed

Two souls with but a single thought,

Two hearts that beat as one.

Maria White Lowell

A Special Invitation

Jesus Christ lived and died so you might be able to enjoy God's presence fully here on earth and for an eternity thereafter. One honest look at human nature makes it clear that our condition stands in the way of that relationship.

...for all have sinned and fall short of the glory of God. – Romans 3:23

Scripture is also clear about the consequences of that condition—and its solution.

For the wages of sin is death, but the free gift of God is eternal life in Christ Jesus our Lord. – Romans 6:23

For God so loved the world, that He gave His only begotten Son, that whoever believes in Him shall not perish, but have eternal life. For God did not send the Son into the world to judge the world, but that the world might be saved through Him. He who believes in Him is not judged; he who does not believe has been judged already, because he has not believed in the name of the only begotten Son of God. – John 3:16-18

Through Christ's sacrifice on the cross, God gave humanity a lifeline and his desire is for all people—including you—to grasp it.

... that if you confess with your mouth Jesus as Lord, and believe in your heart that God raised Him from the dead, you will be saved; for with the heart a person believes, resulting in righteousness, and with the mouth he confesses, resulting in

salvation. For the Scripture says, "Whoever believes in Him will not be disappointed." – Romans 10:9-11

(Jesus speaking)"Therefore everyone who confesses Me before men, I will also confess him before My Father who is in heaven. But whoever denies Me before men, I will also deny him before My Father who is in heaven." – Matthew 10:32-33

Don't wait another day or another minute to seek forgiveness at the feet of Jesus, believe he died to give you life, and begin living in unity with him. If you made that decision today, talk to a friend, pastor, or other spiritual mentor about it. And know the angels in heaven are rejoicing over you!

... there is joy in the presence of the angels of God over one sinner who repents. – Luke 15:10

Topical Index by Day

Don't miss out!

Click the button below and you can sign up to receive emails whenever Traci Matt publishes a new book. There's no charge and no obligation.

Sign Me Up!

https://books2read.com/r/B-A-YZPD-XMQN

Connecting independent readers to independent writers.

About the Author

Traci Matt is a journalist, editor, retired homeschooler, and Christ follower. She experienced the thrills and stresses of her three children's weddings over the course of six years, each unique in its beauty and challenges. During that time their home was filled with ribbons and bows, laughter and tears, and the urgent need for a mother's prayers. Today she and her husband live in the Kansas City area in gleefully close proximity to their children and grandchildren. For more information about Traci and her work, including her best-selling book, *Don't Waste Your Time Homeschooling: 72 Things I Wish I'd Known,* visit tracimatt.com.

Made in the USA
Las Vegas, NV
28 November 2021